MORE MATHEMATICAL ACTIVITIES

A resource book for teachers

Brian Bolt

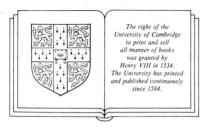

The right of the
University of Cambridge
to print and sell
all manner of books
was granted by
Henry VIII in 1534.
The University has printed
and published continuously
since 1584.

CAMBRIDGE UNIVERSITY PRESS

Cambridge

London   New York   New Rochelle

Melbourne   Sydney

Published by the Press Syndicate of the University of Cambridge
The Pitt Building, Trumpington Street, Cambridge CB2 1RP
32 East 57th Street, New York, NY 10022, USA
10 Stamford Road, Oakleigh, Melbourne 3166, Australia

First published 1985

Printed in Great Britain at the
University Press, Cambridge

British Library cataloguing in publication data

Bolt, Brian
More mathematical activities.
1. Mathematical recreations   2. Puzzles
I. Title
793.7′4
ISBN 0 521 31951 X   QA95

RD

CONTENTS

Page numbers in *italics* refer to the commentary. An asterisk indicates that a calculator is needed.

PREFACE

This book has been written in response to the enthusiastic reception given to my earlier book *Mathematical Activities* which was written to provide teachers with a readily available resource of ideas to enrich their teaching of mathematics. That book contained a mix of investigations, puzzles, games and practical activities, together with a commentary, to stimulate mathematical thinking. That format was clearly approved of, so it has been retained.

The emphasis in the early activities is on spatial thinking, with details of interesting models to make from fascinating folding polyhedra and linkages to harmonographs. Chess board tours, matchstick puzzles, coin puzzles, shunting problems, ways to produce ellipses, parabolas and other curves continue themes introduced in the earlier book but can be attempted independently. The activity on building a matchbox computer can be seen on one level as fun, but has much significance in terms of artificial intelligence. Rigid structures in two and three dimensions have endless possibilities for linking model building in the classroom with structures in the real world, and a box of drinking straws goes a long way!

The calculator is now accepted as the main aid to computation, so several puzzles and investigations have been designed to exploit this. Games too have been designed to encourage the estimation of answers before using the calculator and these have proved very successful.

Apart from a small number of activities little formal mathematical knowledge is required, but the ability to think creatively and mathematically will be essential. Many of the activities in this book have been attempted by a very wide range of people from upper junior school children in a mathematics club to students training as mathematics teachers and experienced teachers on inservice courses. Without the feedback, encouragement and ideas they have all given me this book would never have been written.

Many groups and individuals have contributed to the success of this book but I would particularly like to acknowledge the support of my family; the interest shown by Rosemary Tennison, my editor; and the cheerful way in which Susan Newall transformed my scrawl into a typed manuscript.

Brian Bolt
University of Exeter
School of Education

1 Make a folding tetrahedron

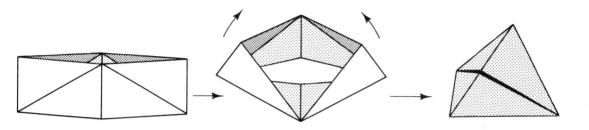

Here is a neat way of making a tetrahedron which can fold flat in an instant. All that is required is a rectangular piece of card 28 cm long and 4 cm wide. Divide the long rectangle into four smaller equal rectangles and mark in the diagonals shown.

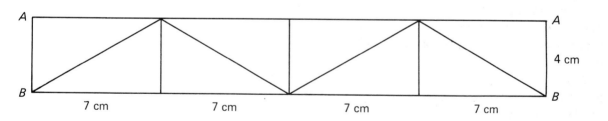

Carefully score all the vertical and diagonal lines using a compass point or pair of scissors. Now join the ends of the long rectangle together using sticky tape to form a band. The band of rectangles can now be folded into the tetrahedron. Easy to make and a very satisfying model to handle.

2 Six pyramids make a cube

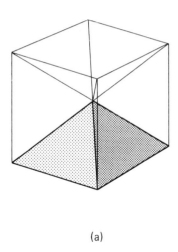

(a)

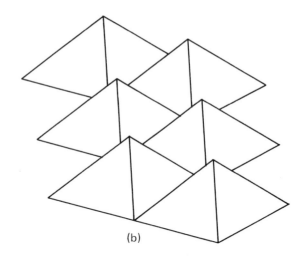

(b)

Consider the pyramid formed by joining the centre of a cube to one of its faces. Clearly, as the cube has six square faces, it can be cut up into six of these pyramids. This is the basis of an attractive model consisting of six pyramids which fold up to form a cube. The pyramids can be made individually and then stuck to a piece of card in the shape of a net of the cube, or, with ingenuity, the net for the whole model can be cut out in one piece. The diagram (b) shows the pyramids joined to form a 'staircase' net of the cube. This is the basis for the net of the model shown on page 3. If you design your own net make sure you have the sides of the triangles in the correct ratio – they are not equilateral, but isosceles with the equal sides being $\frac{1}{2}\sqrt{3}$ times the length of the base. This can be seen by looking at the pyramid inside the cube in diagram (a), where it can be seen that the length of the slant edge is half that of the diagonal of the cube. In practice suitable lengths to take are 5 cm for the length of a side of a square and 4.3 cm for the equal sides of the isosceles triangle.

The net on page 3 may be used by first tracing it accurately, and then copying it onto card by pricking through the tracing paper onto the card at all the intersections. Alternatively, if you have access to a good photocopier, the net can be copied directly onto card. However, it is more instructive and more satisfying to construct your own net.

2

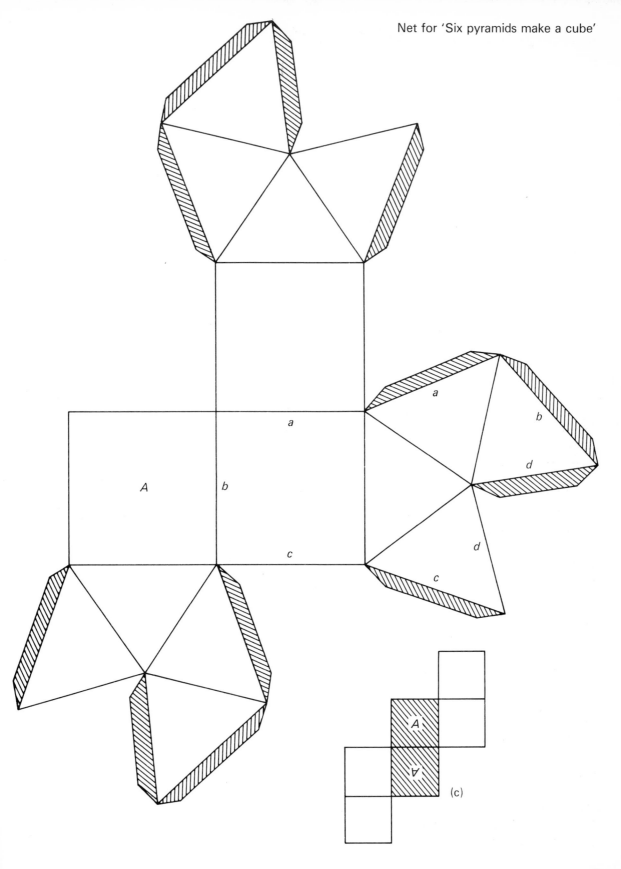

a

A   b

c

a

b

d

d

c

A

A

(c)

The net makes three pyramids so it must be made twice. Score all the fold lines carefully and use a good quick drying glue. When you have made the two sets of three pyramids join the two bases marked A to form the 'staircase' pattern as shown in (c), using a piece of card the size of two squares.

This model can be folded in two distinct ways. First, with the points of the pyramids folded towards the centre it forms a cube. Secondly, with the points of the pyramids folded outwards, and the bases of the pyramids folded to surround a cube, it forms the solid known as a rhombic dodecahedron. This solid has twelve faces all of which are rhombuses made from two triangular faces of adjacent pyramids. The rhombic dodecahedron is one of the very few solids which can be made with congruent faces and it occurs naturally as the shape of the cell in a honeycomb and as a crystal because of its symmetry and space filling properties.

Compare the volumes of the pyramids and the rhombic dodecahedron with the cube on which they were based.

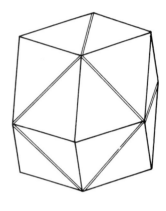

(d) Rhombic dodecahedron

3 Three pyramids make a cube

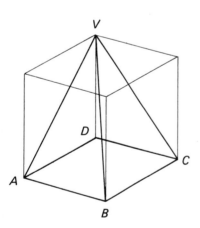

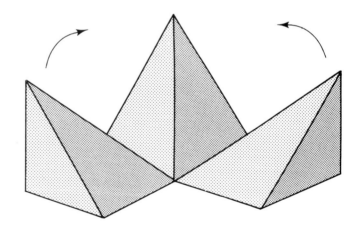

Another interesting dissection of the cube is into three identical pyramids, like $ABCDV$ shown above. This pyramid is not symmetric like those of the previous model but has its vertex immediately above a corner of the square base. This makes two of its triangular faces, ADV and CDV in the diagram, exactly half of two square faces of the cube. The remaining two faces ABV and CBV are right-angled triangles whose sides are equal to a side of the square, a diagonal of the square and a long diagonal of the cube, so they are easy to construct.

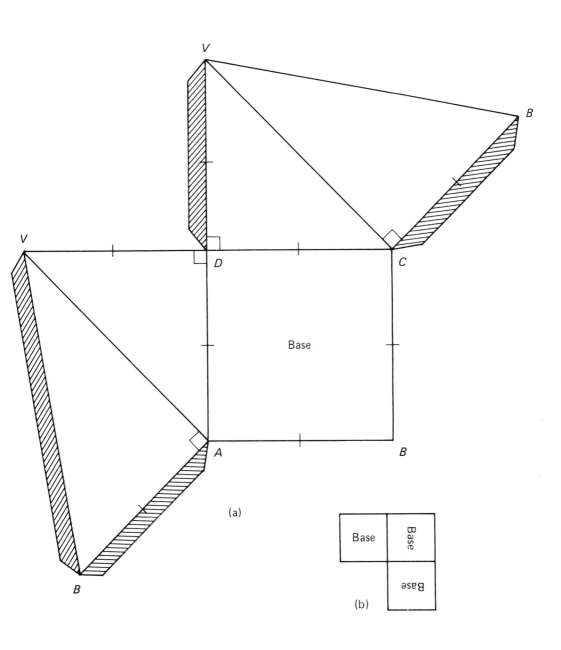

(a)

Base

(b)

The first time you make this model it is easier to make three identical pyramids using net (a) and join them with sticky tape or stick them to an L-shape piece of card (b) made from three squares with the base in the directions shown. However, it is an interesting challenge to design a net for the three pyramids in one.

4 The Shinsei Mystery

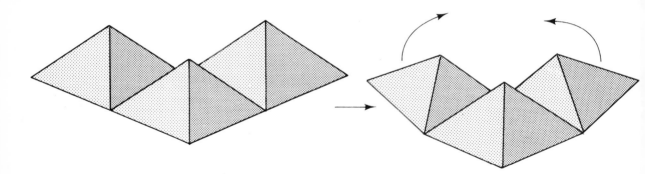

In 1982 a mathematical toy was marketed called 'The Shinsei Mystery'. It comes as two identical parts each of which is made up of eight hinged polyhedra and is capable of being manipulated into many fascinating shapes, including a cube and a solid 12-pointed star.

If you don't already possess this model then look out for it, but meanwhile you can make your own version from card.

The basis of this model is the half-cube (right) which is best visualised by starting with three of the pyramids for the model described in activity 2 and folding them so that their vertices meet in the middle of the cube. A net for the resulting half-cube is given on page 7. For strength, one of the triangular faces occurs twice in this net and these should be stuck together.

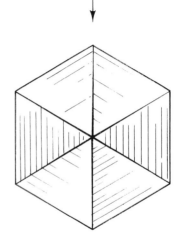

Each half of The Shinsei Mystery consists of eight of these half-cubes cleverly hinged together. They are shown folded to form the symmetric 12-pointed star in (a). But to show how they are hinged, it is easier to consider them in the flatter arrangement which can best be described as cutting the star in half horizontally, and placing the identical halves side by side.

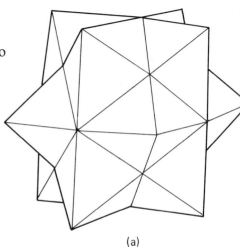

(a)

Half a cube (Shinsei Mystery)

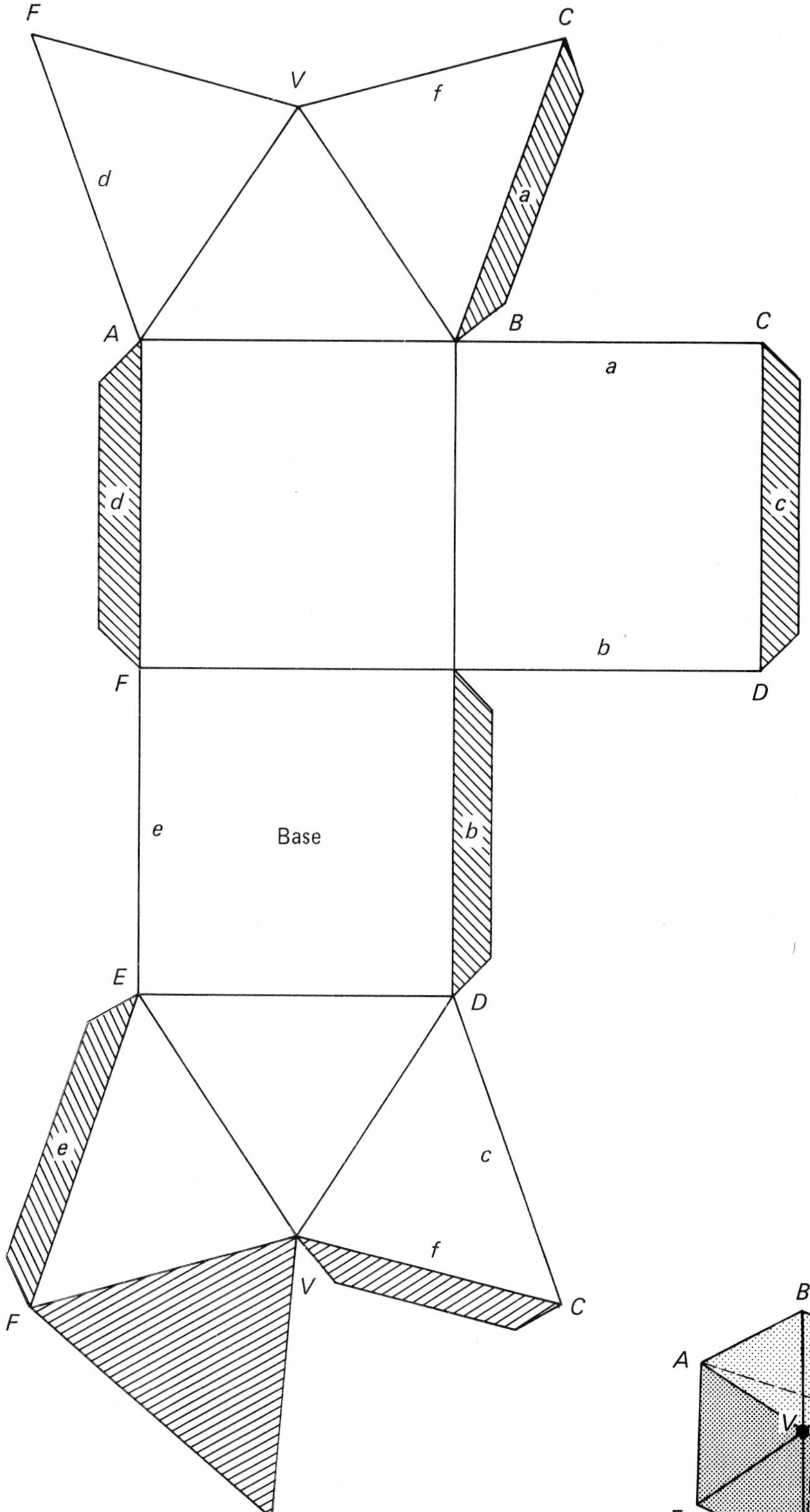

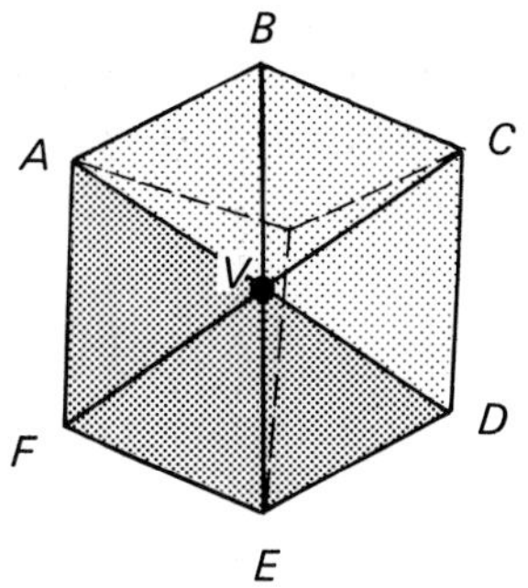

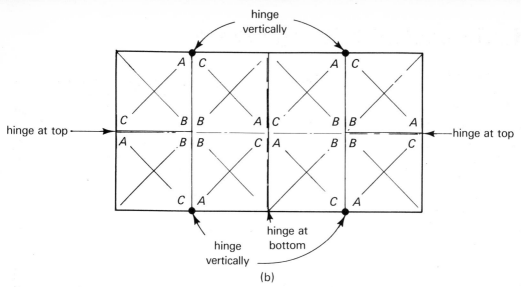

hinge
vertically

(b)

(b) shows the view from above and the letters *A*, *B*, *C* correspond to the lettering on the half-cube net on the previous page. Place eight half-cubes with their square bases *DEF* on a flat surface in this arrangement and then make hinges with sticky tape as indicated. You should now find you have a model which will fascinate you and everyone who handles it. Make a second one like it in a different colour and you will find they can be made to fit together in such a way that as they are manipulated one disappears inside the other.

5 The car jam

In a small underground private car park in the centre of London the cars were packed in like sardines. So tightly were the cars parked that the only way a car could be moved was to push it forwards or backwards along its length. The car marked 1 in the diagram belonged to the managing director of the firm owning the car park. He was in a hurry to get out! Help the car park attendant by finding the minimum number of car moves required for car 1 to be released from the jam it is in.

A set of dominoes makes a very handy visual aid when trying to solve this puzzle.

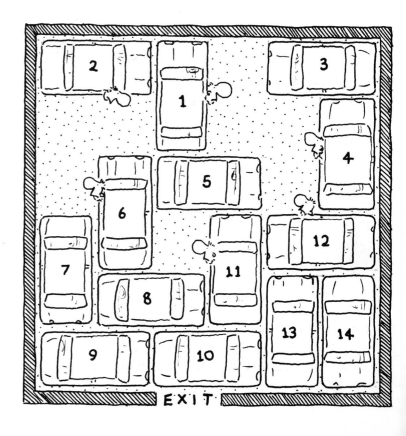

6 The flight controller's nightmare

With the increase in package-holiday flights to the continent, a flight controller was responsible for trying to route safely an ever-increasing number of planes from the south of England to the continental resorts.

One particularly vexing problem was caused by three large companies who operated out of airports *A, B* and *C* respectively and who each wanted direct flights to the airports at *P, Q* and *R*. Because of the high density of traffic on these routes it was important that none of the flight paths should cross. Flying over an airport is quite out of the question. Can you find nine flight paths to solve the controller's problem?

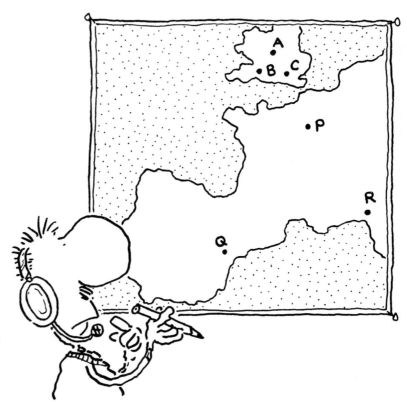

7 The vanishing act

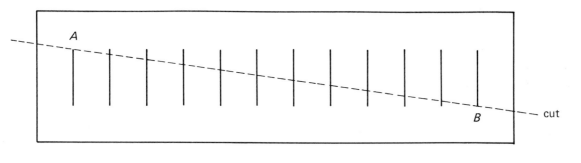

(a)

On a sheet of paper carefully draw twelve lines each 3 cm long and 2 cm apart as shown. Then carefully cut the paper into two along the line *AB* which joins the top of the first line to the bottom of the last line.

9

Now slide the two pieces of paper along the cut edge until the lines first coincide as in the next diagram.

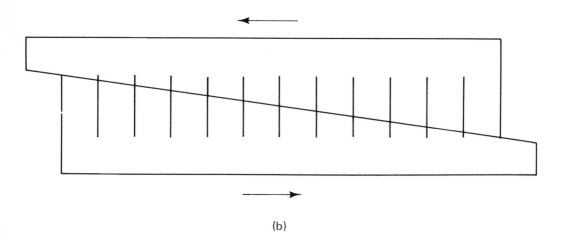

(b)

How many lines are there now? How can you account for the apparent discrepancy?

8 Mystifying matchsticks

Take away four matchsticks to leave exactly four equilateral triangles all of the same size.

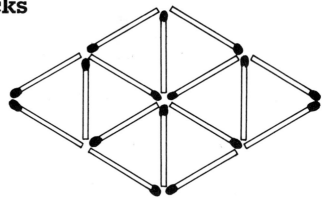

9 Calculator cricket

This is a game for two players which has been designed to improve skills of estimating answers before using a calculator.

In essence, the game consists of one player (the batsman) setting a sum, the second player (the bowler) then estimating the answer, and a calculator then being used to find the difference between the correct answer and the estimated answer. This difference is then the batsman's score.

Clearly the sums allowable must be carefully defined before play begins and at a level to suit the ability of the players so that the differences between correct and estimated answers give acceptable scores. For example, at one level of ability the sums could be confined to the product of two 2-digit numbers. A game then consists of the player representing the batting side setting eleven sums, and the player representing the fielding side trying to restrict the score by estimating the answers as accurately as possible. When one side has batted the players reverse roles, with the winner being the player with the highest aggregate score.

It is helpful if the sums and estimates are set out in an orderly way such as the following:

Batsman's sums	Bowler's estimations	Calculator products	Score
23×47	1000	1081	81
38×57	2200	2166	34
71×29	2100	2059	41
86×94	8100	8084	16

Initially the scores may be astronomical, but as the skill of the estimator improves, and there is every incentive in this game for that to happen, the score of the batting side is reduced.

Have a go; it's fun!

10 Generating straight-line motion

With the development of steam power and many complex machines in the industrial revolution the ability to convert circular motion into motion along a straight line was of prime importance to engineers. The result was that many engineers and mathematicians of the period put a lot of effort into solving this practical problem. The solutions of Watt and Tchebycheff were discussed in *Mathematical Activities* but there are many others of interest. Perhaps the best known is that by a French army officer named Peaucellier who published his solution in 1864.

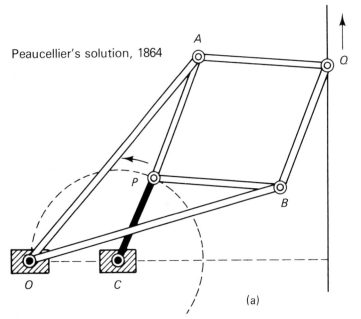

Peaucellier's solution, 1864

(a)

He used a linkage consisting of four equal bars joined to form a rhombus (*AQBP* in the diagram), and two longer bars of equal length joining opposite corners of the rhombus to a fixed point *O*. This linkage has the property that whenever the point *P* is constrained to move on a circle through *O* then the point *Q* will travel along a straight line. In diagram (a) this has been achieved by attaching *P* to a bar which can rotate about a fixed point *C* where the distance of *C* from *O* is equal to the length of *CP*.

The proof that this mechanism produced straight-line motion is beyond the scope of this book, but by far the best way to appreciate this mechanism, and the ones that follow, is to make it. If you have geostrip or Meccano it will be a simple matter, but very satisfactory results can be obtained using strips of thick card and brass paper fasteners.

Theoretically Peaucellier's solution gives an exact straight-line, but with any slackness in the joints it easily departs from its appointed path. However, a solution proposed by Roberts in 1860 gives a very good approximation to straight-line motion and is more practical.

It consists of a triangular metal plate *BCP* connected to two fixed points *A* and *D* by two rods *AB* and *DC*.

$$AB = BP = DC = CP \text{ and}$$
$$AD = 2BC.$$

While *P* moves between *A* and *D* it appears to be on an exact straight line but when *P* moves outside of *AD* it soon diverges from it to the point where *AB* and *DC* cross when *BPC* is above *BC*.

Again, an easy model to make with card and well worth the effort.

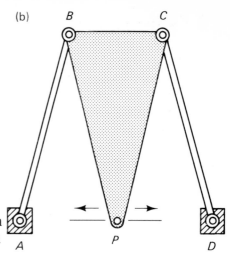

Roberts' solution, 1860

A third solution is shown in diagram (c). Here a circular roller rolls around the inside of a circle twice its diameter. The result is that any point such as *P* on the circumference of the roller traces out a diameter of the large circle, *AB* in the diagram. As the roller turns anticlockwise from the position 1 the point *P* moves towards *B* and reaches *B* when the roller touches the circle at this point. Then *P* starts moving towards *A* as the roller continues around the circle.

A model of this can easily be made with thick card but owners of the Spirograph toy will find it a very easy model to construct.

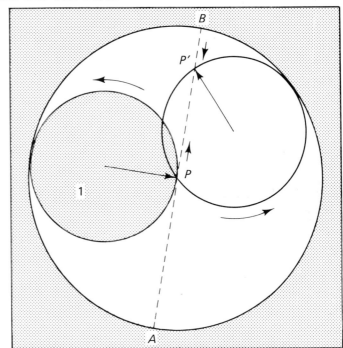

(c)

What happens to a chord of the rotating roller such as *MN* in the course of the revolution?

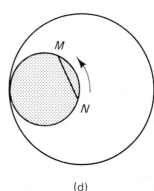

(d)

One of the most widely used sources of power for over a hundred years was the Cornish beam engine, and it was an impressive sight with its large heavy cast iron beam oscillating slowly up and down.

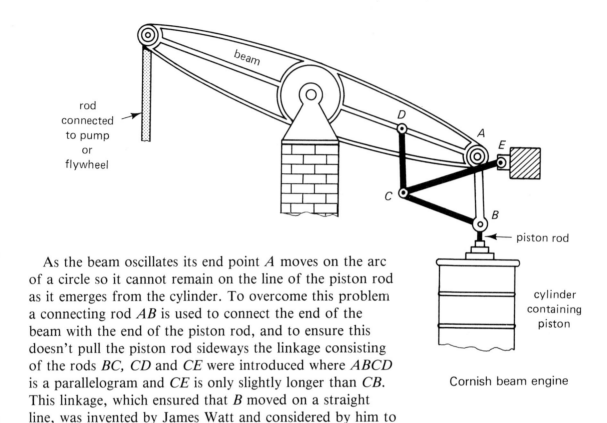

Cornish beam engine

As the beam oscillates its end point A moves on the arc of a circle so it cannot remain on the line of the piston rod as it emerges from the cylinder. To overcome this problem a connecting rod AB is used to connect the end of the beam with the end of the piston rod, and to ensure this doesn't pull the piston rod sideways the linkage consisting of the rods BC, CD and CE were introduced where ABCD is a parallelogram and CE is only slightly longer than CB. This linkage, which ensured that B moved on a straight line, was invented by James Watt and considered by him to be his greatest achievement.

11 Make a mobile to defy gravity

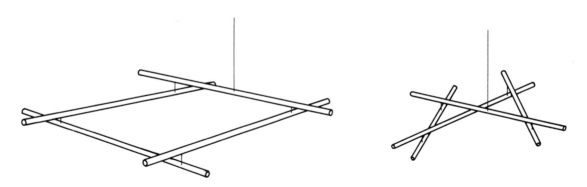

This simple mobile, which in one position looks like a parallelogram, moves in the lightest air current in a fascinating way. It is made from four straws (preferably extra long ones such as can be purchased in handicraft shops), and, by careful 'weighting', the straws will remain horizontal apparently defying the laws of gravity as it moves into different configurations.

The straws are suspended below each other by very fine black cotton or fishing line, to be as invisible as possible. The cotton is threaded through small holes made through the straws about $\frac{1}{5}$ of the distance from each end using a fine needle, and the straws are carefully arranged to come under each other as the diagram indicates.

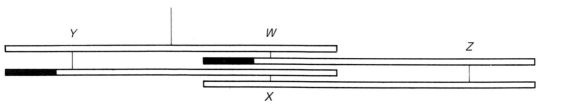

The cotton at W and X is kept as short as possible compatible with the straws not coming into contact, and then the length of the cotton at Y and Z is adjusted to make all the straws parallel when the mobile is lying on a flat surface.

The top straw is suspended from the ceiling at its midpoint and without 'weighting' the mobile would hang down lifelessly. However, by carefully experimenting, weights can be inserted inside the two middle straws at their ends nearest the top straw (indicated by black on the diagram) to balance the mobile so that all the straws stay horizontally in space. The author used nails for this purpose, inserted inside the straw and held in place with blue-tack. When the balance is almost right fine adjustments can be made by adding or subtracting blue-tack to either end of the middle straws. To really baffle your friends, seal the ends of all the straws with blue-tack so that it is not obvious how gravity is defied!

12 The triangular building site

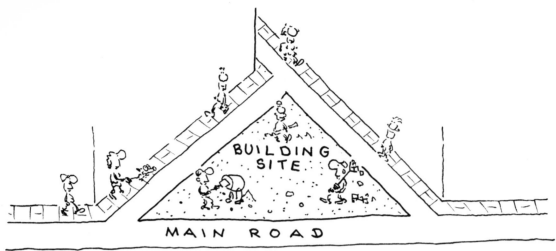

A builder acquired planning permission to erect three
detached houses on a triangular building plot bounded by
three roads. To make the best of the site the builder
proposed to divide it into three triangular sites each having
the same area.

How can this be done?

13 Ring the triangle

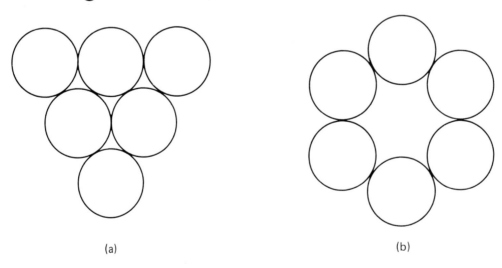

(a)   (b)

Make a triangle of six pennies as shown in (a). What is the
smallest number of pennies you can move by sliding to
form the ring of pennies as in (b), if every time a penny is
moved it must be put into contact with two other pennies?
Note you are not allowed to push one coin with another.

14 K9 or One man and his dog

This is a puzzle based on the traditional problem of finding
a route for a knight to follow on a chess board which visits
each square of the chess board once only. See activity 89 in
Mathematical Activities if you are not familiar with
knight's tours.

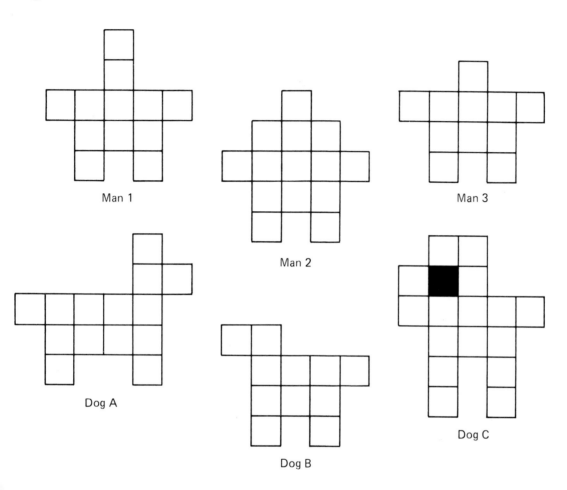

Man 1

Man 2

Man 3

Dog A

Dog B

Dog C

   The drawing depicts three men and three dogs, and the
object is to pair them off correctly. To do this you must
investigate knight's tours on these shapes and decide on
which it is

    (i) impossible to find a tour
   (ii) possible to find a tour
  (iii) possible to find a re-entrant tour.

Note that a re-entrant tour is defined as a route which a
knight could follow around the shape, visiting each square
once, and ending up a knight's move from its starting
square.

15 The anti-litter campaign

The city councillors were becoming very concerned about
the amount of litter being left in their very beautiful park.
To combat this they decided to instal a number of litter
bins as strategically as possible. The park was criss-crossed
in an intricate way by fourteen straight paths, as shown in
the plan above, and the city fathers recommended that
there should be a minimum of 3 litter bins on each path.
The city treasurer protested at the likely cost, for he
supposed it would require $14 \times 3 = 42$ bins, so he was
pleasantly surprised when the park keeper showed him that
the requirement could be met with far fewer bins.

What is the smallest number of bins required, and where
should they be placed?

How many park attendants would be required to ensure
that there is one on every path?

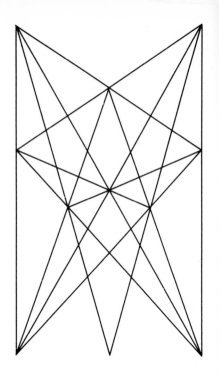

16 The railcar terminus

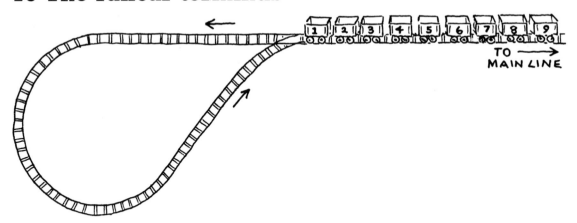

Many different railcar routes converged at an important
city station which formed the terminus for the lines. This
terminus differed from most others however in that it did
not have a multiplicity of sidings but, instead, had a single
loop at the end of the track (see the diagram). The railway
engineer who designed the layout was praised for his
economic use of land and the ingenious way in which the
loop allowed the order of the railcars arriving at the station
to be permuted for different departure patterns. Show how
to use the loop to change the order of nine railcars which

arrive in the order 1, 2, 3, 4, 5, 6, 7, 8, 9, so that they can depart in the order 7, 9, 8, 1, 2, 4, 5, 3, 6. Note that the loop is long enough to contain all the railcars together, if necessary, and that the railcars can travel around the loop in an anticlockwise direction.

Devise a strategy for the controller of the railcars which will enable him to achieve any order he requires.

17 Paving the patio

A keen gardener planned a new patio, in the form of a square, using 64 paving slabs. To add interest, he used an equal number of paving slabs in each of four colours. After much experimenting he ended up with a design which consisted of four identical interlocking shapes, one in each colour.

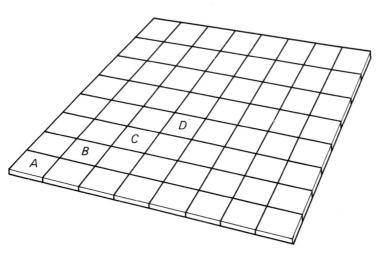

Each of the paving slabs labelled *A, B, C* and *D* in the diagram was a different colour. What was the design?

18 Make a twistable tetrahedral torus

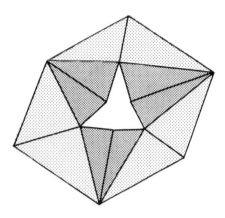

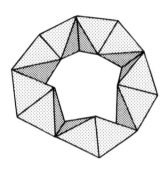

The drawings above are of two fascinating models which consist of rings of tetrahedrons which can be twisted round and round like smoke rings. Adjacent tetrahedrons in the ring are joined along one edge which acts as a hinge, while any single tetrahedron, such as *ABCD,* in the ring is attached to its neighbours by a pair of its opposite edges such as *AB* and *CD* in the diagram. It is this which gives the ring its twistable property.

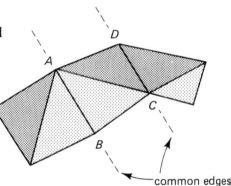

These rings can be made by first constructing a number of congruent tetrahedrons and then joining them by their edges using sticky tape. However, they lend themselves to being made from a single net consisting of a double band of triangles.

A full-size net is given for the ring of six tetrahedrons on page 21. It consists of 24 identical isosceles triangles, 4 for each tetrahedron. When making the model for the first time label the tabs and the places where they are to join very carefully to aid in its construction. Score all the lines and note that the card has to bend upwards or downwards depending on whether the lines are solid or broken. When sticking the net together, it is easiest to concentrate first on a strip of triangles near the middle like those shaded from *d* to *d*. These triangles fold together to form a tetrahedron and when you have managed that satisfactorily, you will find the remaining tetrahedrons easily fold into place. Joining the ends of the ring together can be tricky, particularly if you make the model on too small a scale, and another pair of hands may be required. The two triangles labelled *i* should completely overlap one another and strengthen the join.

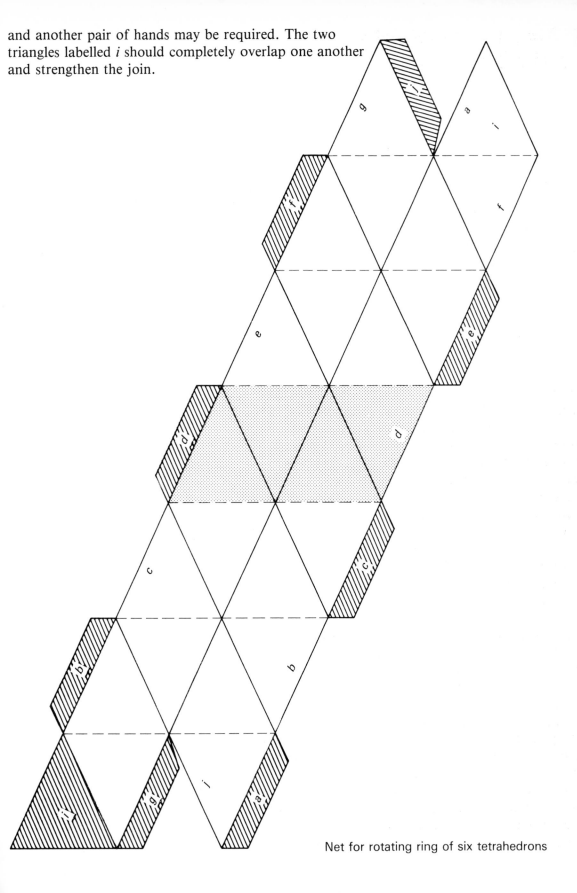

Net for rotating ring of six tetrahedrons

The completed ring can be painted or coloured by sticking gummed paper to the faces of the tetrahedrons in an appropriate pattern to enhance its appearance.

The nets for a ring of 8, and a ring of 10, tetrahedrons are shown below. This time the triangles are equilateral so it is not difficult to reproduce their nets to whatever scale you like.

Ring of eight tetrahedrons

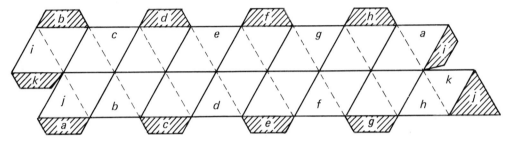

Ring of ten tetrahedrons

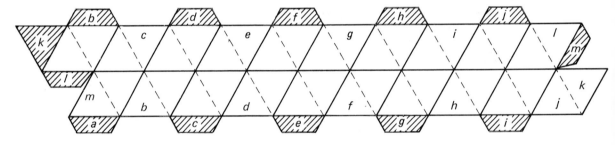

19 Seeing is believing!

We are trained to interpret certain kinds of two-dimensional drawings as representing three-dimensional objects, and the ability to understand such diagrams and to draw them is an aid to thinking and communicating ideas about space. However, as the drawings illustrate, visual impossibilities can be created. Is the first drawing a 3-pin or a 2-pin plug? Can a staircase join up on itself? Could you make the triangle from three pieces of wood?

Visual perception is more the area of study of the psychologist than the mathematician, but diagrams are widely used by mathematicians to help in thinking about space so their shortcomings need to be recognised.

The Dutch artist M C Escher made great play of creating impossible worlds based on the illusions in the drawings. See, for example, his lithographs entitled 'Waterfall', or 'Ascending and Descending', or 'House of Stairs', in *The Graphic Work of M.C. Escher*.

Keep a lookout for drawings which deceive the eye and make a collection of them.

20 Spot the pattern

At a first glance there may seem to be no rhyme or reason in the pattern of black and white circles. But the pattern is generated from the top row, by a simple rule where each new row is worked out from the row immediately above it.

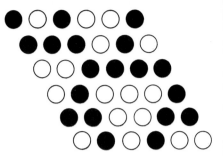

When you have spotted the pattern complete several more rows and see if you can decide whether a row could ever consist of:

    all white circles
    all black circles
    one black circle.

Does the pattern in a row ever repeat itself?
  Investigate what happens starting off with

    (*a*) a different pattern of circles in the first row,
    (*b*) a different number of circles in the first row.

21 Investigations on a 5×5 pinboard

(*a*) On a 5×5 pinboard show that with one elastic band there
    (i) is one way of forming a square surrounding 5 pins.
    (ii) are two ways of forming a symmetric cross each of which surrounds 5 pins.
    (iii) three ways of forming a square which surrounds 9 pins.

(*b*) Using two elastic bands it is possible to form a square which surrounds 5 pins, and has 20 pins outside it.
    Show how to do this.
(*c*) Is it possible to start at a pin, and moving only up and down, and right and left, visit each pin once and end up at the starting pin?

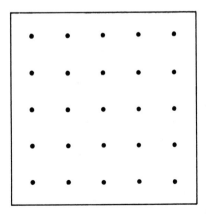

22 Chess board tours

Although the activities here are described in terms of a chess board and chess pieces all that is required is some squared paper, a pencil, and the basic knowledge of how a chess piece moves.

Rook's tours

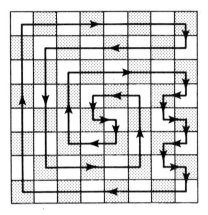
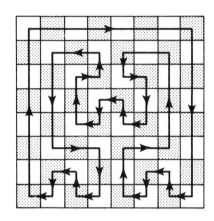

A rook can move to right or left, or up or down only. Investigate routes which a rook can follow on a chess board which enable it to visit every square once and return to its starting point. Such routes, which form continuous loops are called re-entrant. Two solutions are given to start you off.

What is the smallest number of changes of direction required by a rook to complete a re-entrant tour?

If a rook's tour is not required to be re-entrant then it can visit each square once with only fourteen changes of direction. Can you find such a route?

Is it possible for a rook to start at one corner, enter every square once, and finish in the opposite corner?

Queen's tours

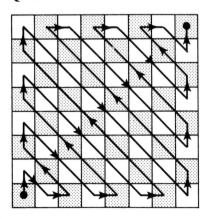
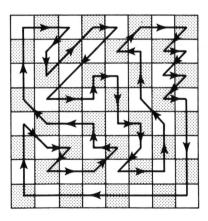

A queen can move diagonally as well as to and fro and up and down like a rook, so its tours can have more variety. The first example of a queen's tour shown here is symmetric and travels from one corner to another, while the second one has no pretence to symmetry but is re-entrant.

Investigate symmetric re-entrant tours.

If the queen is allowed to visit a square more than once then it is possible for her to make a re-entrant tour of the board with only thirteen changes of direction. See if you can find such a solution.

The queen's tour shown right has the fascinating property that if the squares are numbered consecutively, as they are visited, starting with 1 in the square marked *S*, then it will be a magic square. Test it for yourself.

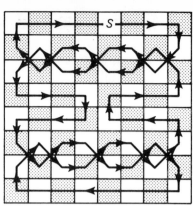

The queen's magic tour

Bishop's tours

Bishops are restricted to diagonal movements only, so if a bishop starts on a black square it can only move to another black square. Even then, it is not possible to visit all the black squares on the board without re-visiting some of them on the way. Why?

The tour shown here misses out on six black squares. You can do better than this!

If you allow the bishop to revisit some squares then it is possible to start at one corner, visit every black square and end in the opposite corner on a route consisting of seventeen lines. How?

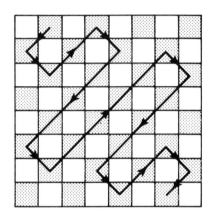

23 Mind stretching

We have all seen a glove or sock turned inside out, and it doesn't need much imagination to see that a ball with a hole cut in it could be turned inside out.

Imagine, however, an inner tube of a bicycle or lorry and imagine cutting a large hole where the valve would be.

By stretching the tube would it be possible to turn it inside out?

It may help you in your deliberations to make a model of the tube, when the hole has been stretched so that there is almost more hole than tube, using two strips of paper coloured to indicate the inside.

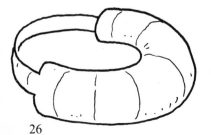

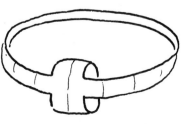

24 One step forward, march!

Imagine 8 knights placed on the black squares of a 4×4 board as shown. Show that they can all manage to make one move.

This is not difficult, but the equivalent problem starting with 13 knights on the black squares of a 5×5 board is a different matter. See what you can make of it!

25 Coin magic

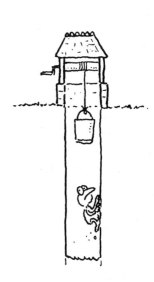

Arrange eight coins as shown to form a square with three coins on each side.

Now move four of the coins to form a square with four coins on each side!

26 The persistent frog

In its search for water a frog fell down a 30 ft well. Its progress out of the well was very erratic. Each day it managed to climb up 3 ft, but the following night it slipped back 2 ft.

How many days does it take the frog to get out of the well?

27 Tidy that bookshelf!

Tidying up the order of books on a library bookshelf is a tedious job so the librarian was always concerned to do it in the most efficient way. She found that the best way to arrive at the order she wanted was by a process of interchanging two books at a time. That is, she would remove any two books from the shelf and replace them in the reverse order.

How many interchanges would she require to place the set of encyclopaedias shown in the order 1 2 3 4 5 6 7 8 9?

What would be the most efficient way if the books had been in the order 4 5 7 6 8 1 9 2 3?

Devise a strategy to find out which interchanges to make for an optimum solution for tidying up the encyclopaedias no matter how they were left.

28 Square a Greek cross

Cut out a Greek cross from a piece of card. Now divide the cross into four pieces with two straight cuts in such a way that the pieces can be rearranged to form a square.

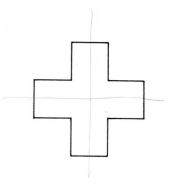

29 The fuel delivery

A large modern city was built with a system of ring roads and link roads as shown. At each of these road junctions the Monopoly Oil Company had a petrol station.

Show that a petrol delivery driver can leave the depot with a tanker and visit each petrol station once and, without passing it again, return to the depot.

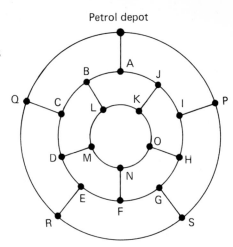

30 Fair shares

A farmer and his friend bought an 8 gallon barrel of cider. They wanted to share the cider equally between them but only had a 5 gallon container and a 3 gallon container. How did they manage?

31 Move a queen

This is a game for two players.

Place a number of queens on a chess board, say five as shown.

Players play alternately.

A move can be either

(a) take a queen off the board

or (b) move a queen any number of squares

    (i) to the left

    (ii) down

    (iii) diagonally down and left.

If, as a result of a move, two queens occupy the same space then both queens are removed from the board.

The winner is the player who removes the last queen.

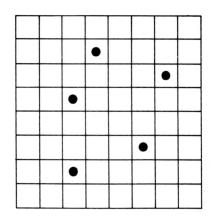

32 Rolling cubes

For this activity you will need a cube. A child's brick
would be fine, but you could manage with a lump of
sugar, or make one from card. On one surface of the cube
mark a large letter A and then place the cube on a board
or paper, covered in squares which match the faces of the
cube as shown. The initial object of this investigation is to
see which squares on the board can be reached, with the A
uppermost facing in its original direction, by rolling.

For example, if the cube is rolled to the right it will need
to be turned about four edges before it is again facing the
right way up on the fourth square to the right of its initial
position. These four moves might be recorded as R_4 or R^4.
It will certainly help your investigations if you invent a
shorthand notation to record your moves.

When you are satisfied you know which squares can be
reached from the initial position and the most efficient way
of achieving it, try your hand at rearranging five cubes,
whose initial position spells WARTS, to the same five
squares, spelling STRAW.

33 Make yourself a harmonograph

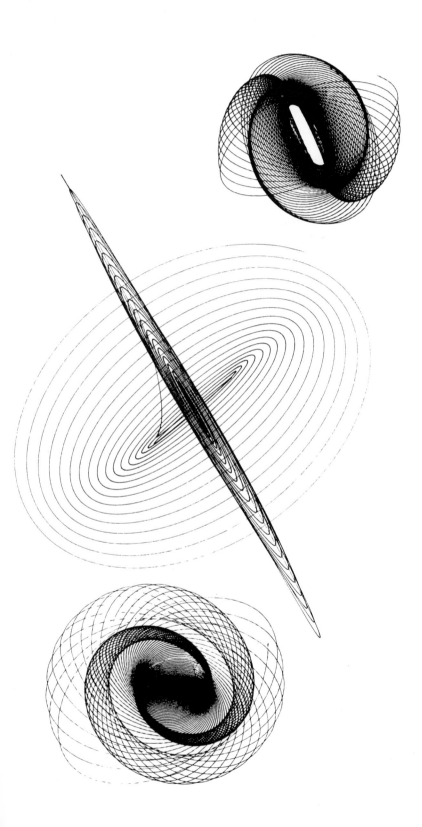

In many Victorian drawing rooms a machine could be found which produced patterns of the kind shown on page 31. These machines, known as harmonographs, depended on the oscillating motion of a pendulum for their effect. They were usually made by skilled craftsmen out of metal, but this is not necessary. Very effective harmonographs can be made, quite simply, by building on a larger scale, and three approaches are described here. The author made the first to be described, in half an hour, from materials found in the garden shed!

The paving slab harmonograph

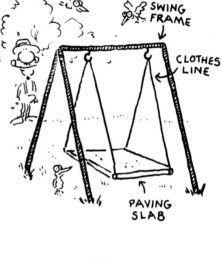

The weight used in the first harmonograph was a paving slab, as used by countless gardeners everywhere. It was suspended by two loops of clothes line from the hooks of a swing frame, as shown, so that it could swing close to the ground. (Two hooks in any handy beam or lintel would do well, or in the branch of a suitable tree.) The paving slab, being flat, was used for the table of the harmonograph, and to make a smoother surface for the paper a piece of hardboard was placed over it. The paving slab was free to oscillate as a conical pendulum, that is, round and round like a conker on a string, not simply to and fro like the pendulum of a clock. It is this motion that is responsible for the attractive patterns produced.

All that remained was to fix a ball-point pen in such a way that it stayed in contact with the table, with sufficient pressure for it to draw, as the paving slab swung around in ever decreasing oscillations. This was achieved by taking a strip of wood about a metre long and screwing it to a second piece about 30 cm long, at right angles to it at its point of balance, to form a cross. See the diagram. A

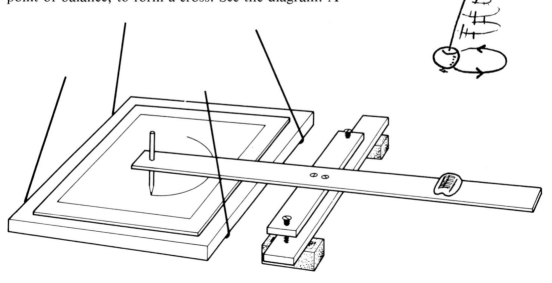

wood screw was then screwed through each end of the cross-piece so that it protruded about 1 cm through the wood to act as a pivot. This pen-arm was then pivoted on a suitably placed piece of wood so that it could see-saw with one end over the centre of the paving slab. A hole was drilled through the end of the arm just large enough to take a ball-point pen, and the pressure of the pen on the paper was adjusted by moving a small stone along the arm as a counterbalance. (NB the cross-piece is necessary to prevent sideways movement of the pen-arm.)

To operate the harmonograph a sheet of paper was placed on the hardboard, centred under the pen, and held in place by some small stones from the flower bed. With the pen-arm tilted so that the pen was not in contact with the paper the paving slab was set in motion. The pen was then tilted to make contact with the paper and the swinging slab did the rest. When the design being traced out had reached a satisfactory point the arm was tilted to raise the pen from the paper.

Different designs can be superimposed on top of one another in the same or different colours to create an endless number of patterns. However, with this simple harmonograph the designs will all be based on versions of elliptical spirals.

The broom handle harmonograph

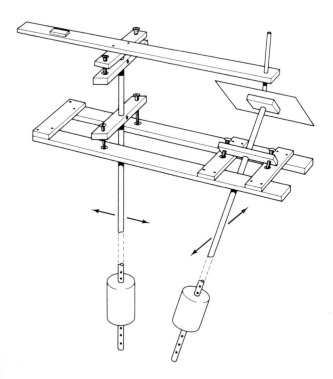

The basis of this harmonograph consists of two broom handles suitably pivoted, and weighted, to form pendulums as shown in the diagram. It was originally made for the author in this way by a group of 12-year-old boys who operated it very successfully. However, it would probably be even more effective if the broom handles were replaced by wooden dowling with a much smaller cross-section, as obtainable in most DIY stores.

The two pendulums swing at right angles to one another. The right-hand pendulum swings from front to back and carries the table to which the paper is fixed. The left-hand pendulum, on the other hand, swings from left to right and carries the pen-arm. This is in contrast to the paving slab harmonograph where the pen is essentially fixed. Further, by varying the heights of the weights on the pendulums their time of swing can be changed relative to one another and this enables more intricate patterns to be produced.

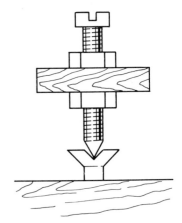

In constructing a harmonograph of this kind try to keep all the moving parts, other than the weights, as light as possible consistent with being rigid. It is also important to have pivots which offer very little resistance to motion so that the pendulums take a long time to come to rest. The author has found that two nuts and a bolt, whose end has been filed to a chisel section and rests in the head of a conventional wood screw, make a very effective pivot which has the added advantage of being adjustable in height.

Each pendulum should be pivoted so that about 25 cm is above the pivot and, say, 75 cm below, but the best height can be found by experiment. The weights on the pendulums need to be as heavy as possible within reason. A heavy piece of metal with a hole through it would be fine, but weights can be made by filling tin cans with concrete. Make the weights with a hole right through them, then they can be slid up and down the rod of the pendulum and fixed at a suitable height by putting a nail through a hole already drilled in the rod.

A Meccano harmonograph

This harmonograph can be constructed by anyone with access to some Meccano. The Meccano parts are used to make a set of 'compass gimbals' to support the pendulum holding the table. The gimbals, see the diagram, allow the table pendulum to swing in any direction, so that the pen arm needs only to move freely in a vertical plane, as with the paving slab harmonograph. The gimbals do not have to be made exactly as shown, but the two gimbal rings need to be made as rigid as possible, yet free to rotate about perpendicular axes without any sideways movement.

A refill from a standard ball-point is an ideal light pen which can be incorporated in a light pen-arm. Consequently the whole harmonograph can be made very compactly and set up in a limited space.

If the pendulum can be pivoted well off the ground then a second conical pendulum can be suspended underneath the first by hanging a weight on a wire attached to a hook in its base. This added complexity leads to much more variety in the possible designs which can be traced, but careful experimenting will be required between the ratios of the weights, and the lengths of the pendulums, to achieve good results.

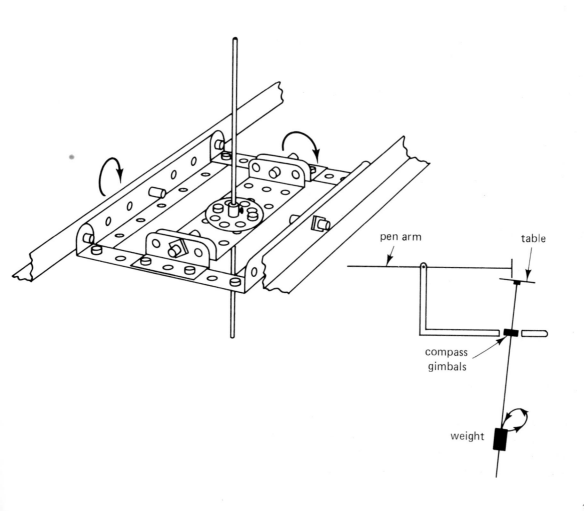

34 Make a matchbox computer

This simple computer 'learns' to play a game by playing against human opponents. Initially it will almost always lose, but, by a process which will be explained, it reaches the point where it almost invariably wins.

Essentially the computer is designed to play a specific game, and to show how the computer works it is first necessary to analyse a game it can play. The game chosen is called Hexapawn and is played on a 3×3 squared board with six pawns – three black and three white.

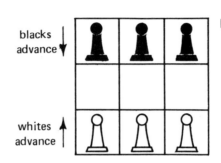

blacks advance ↓

whites advance ↑

Hexapawn board showing starting position

The game starts with the three black pawns and three white facing one another from opposite sides of the board as shown. The pawns move as in chess; that is, they can move one square forward into an unoccupied square, or one square diagonally to capture a pawn of the opposite colour, which is then removed from the board. The diagram shows two possible moves by white in the middle of a game.

A game is won when a pawn reaches the opposite side of the board, or when an opponent's pawns have all been captured, or when an opponent has been put in a position where he cannot move. The following sequence of diagrams depicts a game where black moves first. Each successive diagram shows the positions of the pieces after the previous move and the arrow indicates the next move.

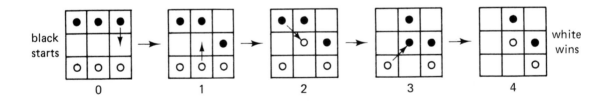

black starts

0 → 1 → 2 → 3 → 4

white wins

You will already have appreciated that this is a very simple game and that very few moves will be required to decide the winner. It has been deliberately chosen, because of this, to keep down the size of the computer. But when you understand, through this game, how it works, you may like to make one to play noughts and crosses, or nim.

But where, you may ask, do matchboxes come in, and how does the computer decide on a move?

The computer consists of a collection of matchboxes, one for every position which the game can take. A diagram showing the position that the matchbox represents is placed on top (see below).

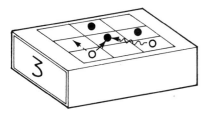

Arrows are drawn indicating *all* possible moves from the positions depicted. In the example drawn here there are three possible moves and these are represented by three different coloured arrows. Inside the box will be beads of the same colour as the arrows. When it is the computer's turn to play, the computer operator selects the appropriate matchbox shakes it and, without looking, takes out a bead. The colour of the bead then indicates the computer's move. Initially the computer is assumed to be a complete idiot and in each matchbox is placed exactly one bead for each possible move — in practice smarties have been found very appropriate for this purpose. The result is that, to begin with, the computer plays many 'silly' moves when you play against it. But it can be 'taught' to play very efficiently by a system of reward and punishment! When the computer loses, as is almost inevitable to start with, it is punished by removing the bead from the matchbox which represented its last move, thus preventing its repetition. If the computer operator comes across an empty matchbox then the computer resigns and a bead representing the last move made is removed. As more and more games are played against the computer it loses its ability to make bad moves, so increases its chances of a win. When it does win it is effectively patted on the back by being given a extra bead in each match box corresponding to its winning moves, further increasing its likelihood of repeating the moves.

All you need to do now to make a computer to play Hexapawn, is to collect as many matchboxes as you can (about forty will be sufficient if you want your computer to be able to play first or second) and to make a careful analysis of all the positions the game can reach. The diagram below is an analysis of all the positions the game can reach in the first three moves, apart from mirror images. You will need a matchbox to represent all these positions and for the positions reached by further moves.

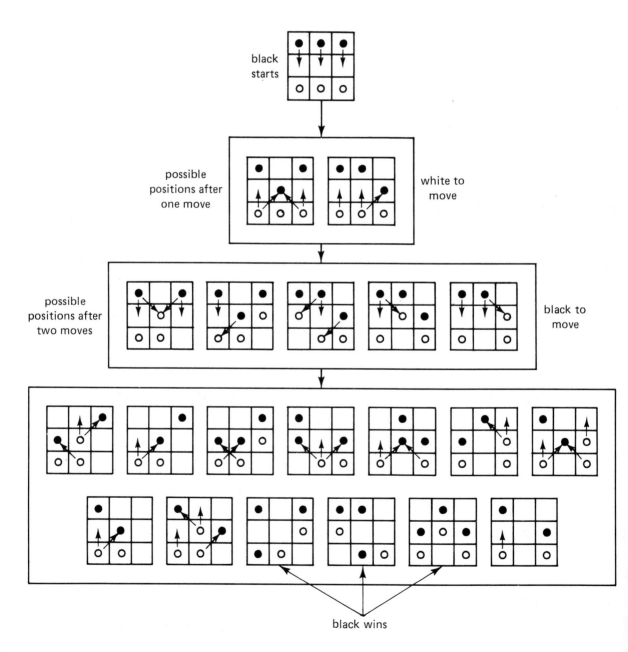

black starts

possible positions after one move

white to move

possible positions after two moves

black to move

black wins

By not having separate matchboxes for mirror images the situation is much simplified and to help their recognition when using the computer it helps to record them both on the matchbox. The two examples given below should make this clear.

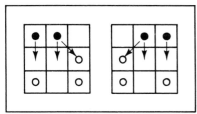 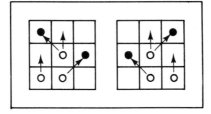

When you have made and instructed your matchbox computer challenge your friends to play it. You might get them to make one too so that the computers can challenge each other.

35 More matchstick mindbenders

Turn the spiral into three squares by moving four matches.

Convert this 'church with tower' symbol into three identical squares by moving five matches.

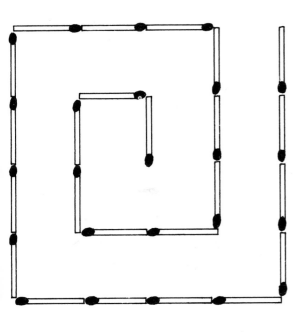 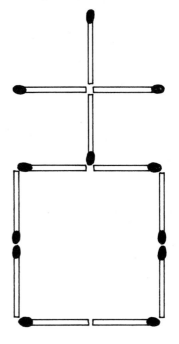

36 Tails up!

The three coin puzzles here are of a kind, but are not all possible. Which is the odd one out?

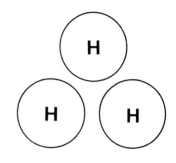

1 Place three coins on the table with head uppermost. A move consists of turning any two coins over. How many moves do you need to arrange for all the tails to be uppermost?

2 Place four coins on the table with heads uppermost. A move consists of turning any three coins over. How many moves do you need to arrange for all the tails to be uppermost?

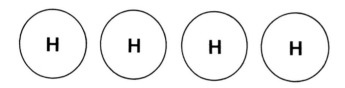

3 Place nine coins in a square array as shown with tails uppermost apart from the coin in the centre. A move consists of turning over the three coins in any row, or any column, or either of the two diagonals. How many moves do you need to arrange for all the tails to be uppermost?

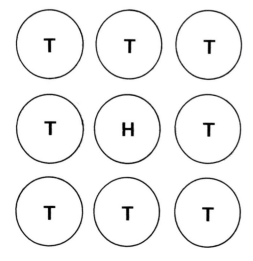

37 Dovetailed

A master carpenter had been teaching his apprentices the art of making dovetail joints. After they had done several routine exercises to perfect their skills he showed them a cube made from two pieces of wood which appeared to have dovetail joints in each of its four vertical faces. The vertical faces all looked identical; see the diagram. The carpenter challenged his apprentices to copy his cube but they were all baffled. It can be made, but how?

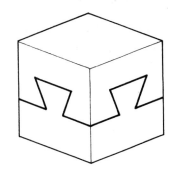

38 Impossible rotations!

Katy challenged her friends to take a book, rotate it through an angle of 180° and then rotate it again through 180° so that the book ends up at 90° to its original position. How can it be done?

39 Problems of single line working

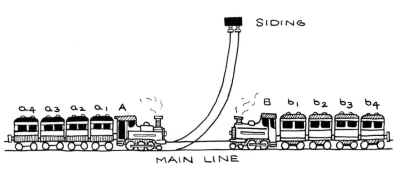

Two passenger trains each with four carriages face one another on a main line. Adjoining the main line is a siding. Unfortunately the siding is only long enough to take an engine and two carriages. Find the most efficient way of shunting the carriages to enable the trains to continue their journey.

40 Solitaire

This is a pegboard game thought to have been invented by a Frenchman while imprisoned in the Bastille in the eighteenth century. Whatever truth there is in the story of its origins, the game has occupied many puzzlers over the years for hundreds of hours.

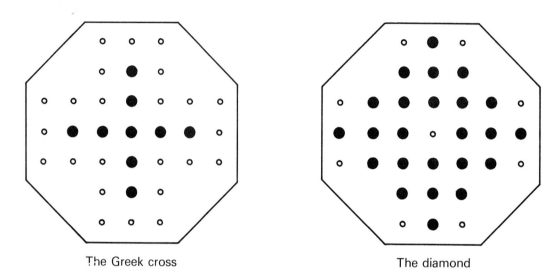

The Greek cross   The diamond

The game is played on a board with holes arranged in the shape of a cross in which pegs are inserted. You could easily make yourself a board to the pattern shown by drilling holes in a block of wood or using pegboard. The diagrams above show pegs inserted in the board for the start of two solitaire games. In both cases the aim is to end up with exactly one peg in the centre hole. The game proceeds by picking up a peg and jumping it over an adjacent peg to an empty hole beyond. The peg which has been leap-frogged is then removed from the board. Only up and down and sideways moves are allowed. Usually a peg having jumped over one peg has nowhere else to go, but skilful players arrange their moves to leave several pegs with spaces between, which then allows a peg to leap-frog these pegs in succession and thus remove more than one peg in a move. In this way the number of moves to reach a final objective can be much reduced. Thus, using these chain moves. The Greek cross can be solved in six moves and the diamond in as few as eight moves.

Some solitaire boards, such as the circular ones shown here, have four additional holes, which leads to further puzzle possibilities. The five crosses arrangement does not

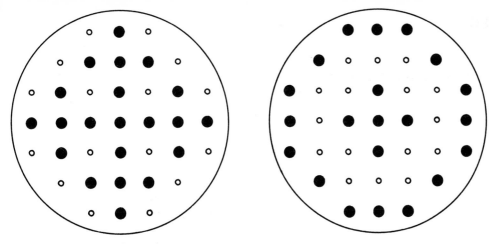

The five crosses   The enclosed cross

use the additional holes in the initial pattern, but no move would be possible without at least one of them. The aim here is to finish with one peg in the centre hole, and this can be achieved in ten moves.

The enclosed cross arrangement shows the *final* position to be achieved from an initial position where there is a peg in every hole except the centre one. This requires at least fourteen moves.

41 All change

Place six coins on a pattern of squares, as shown, so that the coins in the top row are head-up and those in the bottom row are tail-up. The object of this activity is to interchange the heads with the tails in the smallest possible number of moves.

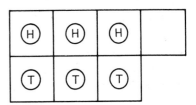

Heads and tails take it in turn to move to any adjacent unoccupied square. A move can be up, down, sideways, or diagonally.

These coins can be interchanged in as few as seven moves. How?

When you have found the solution try solving a similar problem wth a row of four heads above a row of four tails. Then see if you can devise a strategy to solve problems of this kind for any number of coins.

If N is the minimum number of moves for interchanging a row of n heads and n tails how are N and n related?

42 Pegs progress

On a 3×3 pegboard place a red peg in one corner, leave
the opposite corner vacant and put blue pegs in all the
remaining holes as in the diagram. A peg can move up or
down, or sideways, but not diagonally into a space next to
it. Jumping is not allowed.

The object is to get the red peg to the top corner,
opposite its starting position in the smallest possible
number of moves.

When you think you have the best possible solution on a
3×3 board try doing the same for a 4×4 board and then a
5×5 board.

By now you will have developed a basic strategy for
moving the red peg to anywhere you want on the board so
see if you can construct a formula in n for the minimun
number N of moves to take the red peg from one corner to
the opposite corner of an $n \times n$ board.

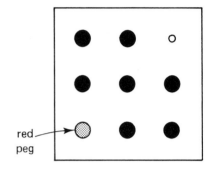

red peg

43 Pinboard triangles

A student teacher on teaching practice was observed giving
a lesson where the children were investigating the different
shapes of triangle they could make on a 3×3 pinboard.
They had found isosceles triangles, right-angled triangles,
acute angled triangles and scalene triangles and were
carefully recording and classifying them. After a while one
child asked 'Will we be able to find an equilateral
triangle?' The student was rather taken aback by this
question but soon convinced himself that it was not
possible on a 3×3 board. However, it raised the question
in his mind of whether it would be possible to find an
equilateral triangle on a larger pinboard, so he gave the
child a 12×12 board with the comment 'No, it is
impossible on a 3×3 board, but you should be able to find
one on this board.'

Was he right?

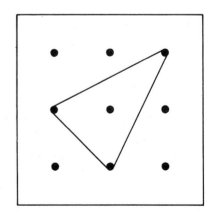

44 Rigid structures in two dimensions

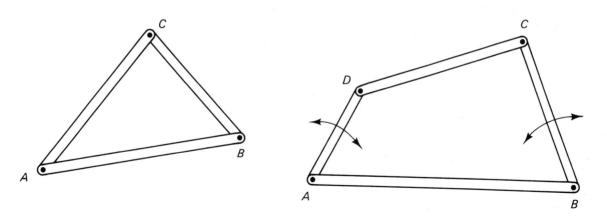

Make a triangle linkage and a quadrilateral linkage from geostrips or card strips using paper fasteners. If you place the linkages on a table and fix *AB* then the point *C* of the triangular linkage is also fixed, but points *C* and *D* of the quadrilateral linkage are free to move. This illustrates the innate rigidity of the triangle linkage, but lack of rigidity in the quadrilateral linkage.

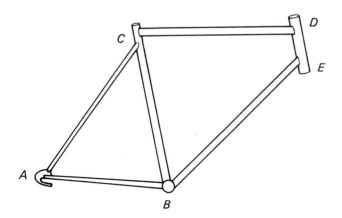

The traditional cycle frame makes use of the triangle's strength at the rear, but the main part of the frame, *BCDE*, which supports the front forks is a fundamentally weak design and relies on the strength of the welded joints. If you are observant you will not have to look far for places where the rigidity of the triangle is used. Look at a deckchair or a folding chair, consider the window fastening which holds a window open, investigate the roof timbers in your house or the structure of a rotating clothes airer. How is the ironing board supported or the garden swing? Look at the design of the traditional farm 5-bar gate. Next time you see scaffolders building their structures of scaffold poles you will see that they introduce a number of diagonal poles to create triangles to make the structure rigid.

Look at the design of crane jibs and railways bridges which are made from linkages. These are structures which have to withstand very heavy loads and often consist of a trellis work of triangles.

Show how to build a bridge across a gap 28 cm wide, using cards strips 8 cm long, jointed only at the ends. A quadrilateral can always be made into a rigid structure by putting in a diagonal strut as shown, turning it into two triangles. Which of the quadrilateral structures shown in the following diagrams are rigid? Make models of them to decide.

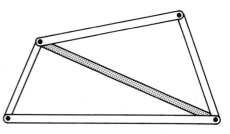

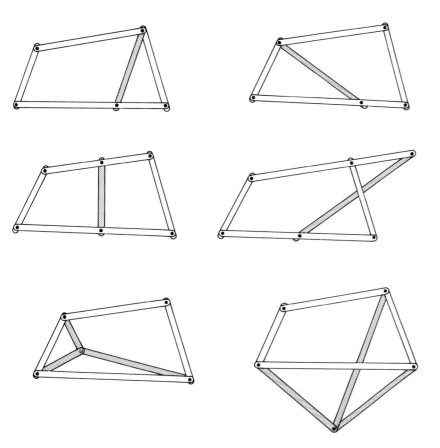

Making these linkages will have given you more ideas on how to make a structure rigid. You should now be in a good position to see how to make a hexagon rigid. Test the following hexagonal structures for rigidity and then investigate ways for yourself of adding struts to make a hexagon rigid.

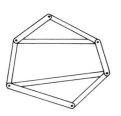
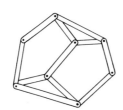
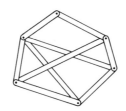

45 Rigid structures in three dimensions

For this activity you require some drinking straws, some thread and a needle. Straws can be joined together to form polygons by feeding the thread through the straws and tying the ends together. The diagram shows a triangle formed in this way.

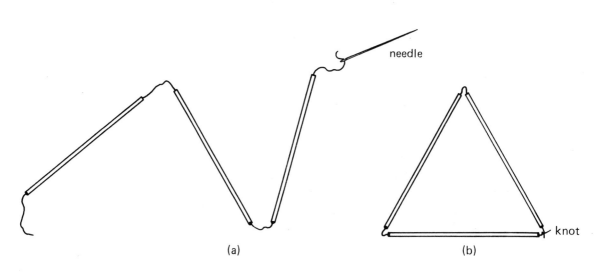

needle

knot

(a)   (b)

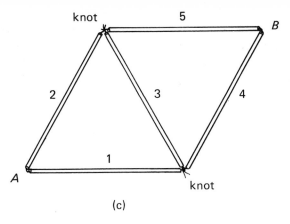

knot 5 B

2 3 4

1

A knot

(c)

If five straws had been threaded in a chain then it would be possible to form two adjoining triangles, as indicated by the numbers in (c).

A sixth straw can now be fitted by hinging the triangles about their common edge, until *A* and *B* are the length of a straw apart, to form a regular tetrahedron (d).

Satisfy yourself that this is a rigid structure even though the 'joints' are flexible.

It is possible to make the tetrahedron with a single piece of thread without having to cut it. How?

The tetrahedron is the simplest three-dimensional rigid structure and plays the same role in three dimensions as the triangle does in two dimensions. Guy ropes attached to flagpoles and television masts often form tetrahedral patterns because of this innate rigidity. Have a look at the base of a folding music stand or consider how a tent stays up. Some dock-side cranes are held in place by timber structures in the form of a tetrahedron. See what other examples you can find of the tetrahedron structure in practice.

Starting with a regular tetrahedron of straws further more complex rigid structures can be formed by adding to it. Just three further straws, for example, leads to two tetrahedrons with a common face. Alternatively, by adding a tetrahedron to each face of the original tetrahedron a four-pointed star is obtained.

By cutting the straws to different lengths, non-regular tetrahedrons can be formed with endless possibilities for combining them and creating interesting rigid three-dimensional structures.

The question now arises as to whether structures not formed from tetrahedrons are rigid.

The square-based pyramid (f) looks rigid enough, and it is as long as it is sitting on a flat surface, but try lifting it up and see what happens. However by adding four more straws to the base of the pyramid to form a second pyramid, which is a mirror image of the first, a rigid structure is obtained. This new structure is in fact a regular octahedron (g).

tetrahedron

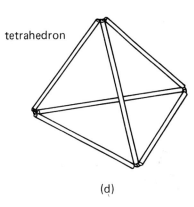

(d)

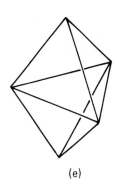

(e)

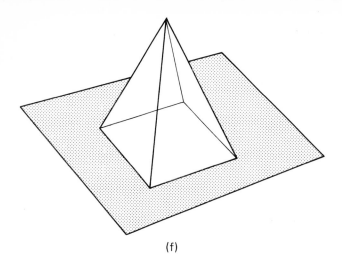

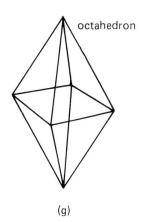

octahedron

(f)

(g)

Turn the completed octahedron around in your hands and note its symmetry — it will look exactly the same no matter which of its six vertices it is suspended from.

How many planes of symmetry does it have?

What shape will be formed if you add a regular tetrahedron to every other face of the regular octahedron?

Now try making a cube by joining straws together using thread. You will soon find how impossibly flexible the structure is. It has the same intrinsic lack of rigidity of structures such as rose pergolas or frameworks to hold nets to keep the birds off soft fruit – it needs diagonals.

It is an interesting problem to investigate different ways of adding further straws to the cube to make it rigid. What will be the smallest number required to do this? One method is to add a pyramid to each face, but this is not the neatest solution.

A note of caution – if you use full length straws for the edges of the cube then you will not have straws of sufficient length to make it rigid!

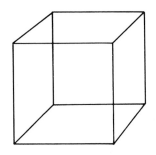

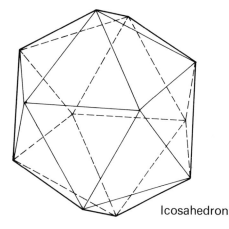

Icosahedron

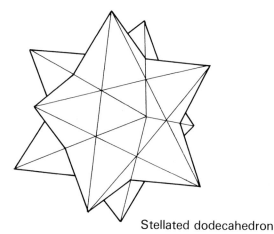

Stellated dodecahedron

One very attractive model to make is the regular icosahedron. This has thirty straws altogether and five straws meet at each of the twelve vertices. It needs some patience to construct for it is not rigid until the last straw is put into place.

If when the icosahedron is complete all its diagonals (exclude the long diagonals joining opposite vertices) are put in using coloured wool, then the stellated dodecahedron is formed inside it. This is a very satisfying model to hang from your ceiling!

The American genius Buckminster Fuller has a world-wide reputation for his invention of the Geodesic Dome, which is a lightweight structure of interlocking triangles used to support a canopy over a large area with no central support. One such dome, for example, had a diameter of 384 feet.

46 A lover's ultimatum!

I ask you, sir, to plant a grove
To show that I'm your lady love.
This grove though small must be composed
Of twenty-five trees in twelve straight rows.
In each row five trees you must place
Or you shall never see my face.

47 Only four lines!

Without taking your pencil from the paper draw four straight lines that together pass through all nine points.

48 Dividing the inheritance

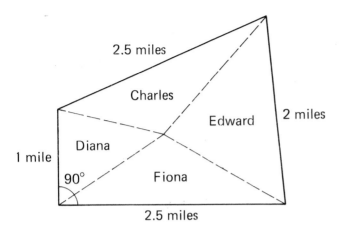

When a sheep farmer in Australia died, he left a will
leaving all his land to his four children Charles, Diana,
Edward and Fiona. To avoid any squabbling over the land
he made a sketch of the ranch, which was in the shape of a
quadrilateral and decreed that the land be divided into four
triangular portions of equal area as indicated.

The initial reaction of the sons was very favourable and
they congratulated their father on his neat solution. It was
only when they tried to put his plan into action that they
realised they had a problem.

What was it?

49 Triangulating a square

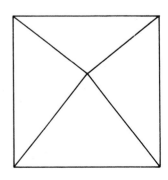

The square shown has been divided up into four triangles.
Only one of these triangles is not acute angled. Is it
possible to divide a square into triangles so that all the
triangles are acute angled? You may use as many triangles
as you think necessary.

50 Who is 'it'?

In a children's game the person to be 'it' was decided by the children standing in a circle and chanting a counting rhyme which had thirteen words. The count went clockwise around the circle successively eliminating every 13th child. There were eight children $a, b, \ldots, h$ and the last child left in was c. Where did the count start?

51 Find the cards on the table

A number of playing cards, all diamonds from one pack, were arranged in a circle on the table in such a way that the total face values of any set of three adjacent cards differed by at most one from the total for any similar set. The highest and lowest cards on the table were the 10 and 2 of diamonds. the 5 and 6 of diamonds were also in the circle.

Which other cards were on the table and what was their order?

52 Reafforestation!

A part of the woodland owned by the forestry commission
needed thinning out. At the start there were 49 fir trees in
a 7×7 array as shown, but by the time the forestry
workers had done their job they had removed 29 trees and
managed to leave 20 trees so that they stood in 18 lines
with 4 trees in each!

How did they do it?

53 The rolling cube game

This is a game in the same tradition as the Rubik
cube. It consists of eight identical cubes, with
each face a different colour, sitting in a tray as
shown, with a space in the centre. To start, the
cubes are put in the tray in a random fashion.
The object of the game is to arrange the cubes so
that the same colour is on the top surface of each
of them by rolling cubes through 90° about a

bottom edge into the vacant space in the tray. At
the start and at the end, the vacant space has to
be in the centre, but clearly the space moves
every time a cube is rolled. A game of patience!

54 Two at a time

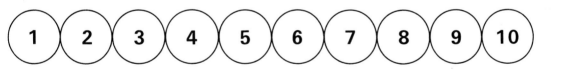

Put ten coins in a line as shown. A move consists of
picking up a coin, leaping over two coins and landing on
another coin. Show that in five moves it is possible to
arrange the coins into five pairs equally spaced. Not as
easy as it seems!

Now allow the possibility of a coin landing in a space as
well as on top of another coin, after jumping over the two
coins, and find what lengths of lines of coins can be
transformed into piles of two. It is no longer necessary for
the piles to be equally spaced. What will be the minimum
number of moves in each case?

55 The prisoner's perambulations

A princess was imprisoned in a castle which was built with four wings around a rectangular courtyard. At each corner was a tower and, for security, the princess was kept in a room in the top floor of one tower. During the day she was allowed to roam freely along the main corridors of the top two floors. A single corridor ran the length of each wing on each floor and there was a staircase in each tower between the floors. To help pass the time the princess amused herself by seeing how many different routes she could walk between parts of the castle accessible to her.

How many different ways could she walk from her room at the top of one tower, to the room on the floor below in the opposite tower, if she did not allow herself to revisit any point of her route, and avoided walking up any staircase?

How many further routes could she have found if she also allowed herself to climb a staircase on the way?

56 Crossed lines

Electricity power lines were constructed from two power stations P_1 and P_2 to three towns T_1, T_2 and T_3. To reduce power losses the grid lines were constructed in straight lines to make them as short as possible. Construction problems arise where two lines cross, which fortunately was only three times in this case (see the crosses on the diagram). It is proposed to connect more power stations to a larger number of towns but before doing so an investigation is required into the number of crossed lines which will arise. For technical reasons, multiple intersections have to be avoided.

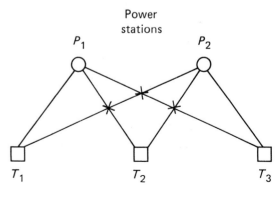

Find the number of crossed lines which will occur when

(*a*) two power stations are each connected to four towns

(*b*) three power stations are each connected to five towns.

Assume that the power stations and towns are on parallel straight lines.

Can you find a formula for the number (n) of crossed lines when p power stations are each connected to t towns.

57 Bridging the river

In an initiative test two teams of army engineers were challenged to build a 'bridge' across a river 5 metres wide. They had an unlimited supply of identical sleepers 4 metres long and could proceed *only* by piling one sleeper upon another.

How far from the bank is it possible for such a structure to reach with only three sleepers?

What is the smallest number of sleepers required to achieve the engineers' objective?

58 Crossing the desert

A fully laden lorry can carry fuel and supplies for a desert journey of 400 miles. At the base camp on the edge of the desert there is a good supply of both. By setting up strategic supply dumps on the proposed route the lorry can travel into the desert and return to base much further than the 200 miles limit which one load would allow.

How many journeys from base would be needed to be able to penetrate 600 miles into the desert and return safely?

59 Can you help the motorway designer?

Four large towns lie at the vertices of a square of side 20 miles. Because of the growing importance of trade between the towns the government decided to design a motorway network to connect all the towns to each other. Naturally, the government wanted to keep the cost to a minimum, so they insisted that the engineers made the motorway as short as possible.

The engineers considered the merit of a variety of solutions, such as the three shown here, and

B ●   ● C

A ●   ● D

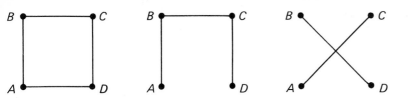

soon came to the conclusion that the best solution would be to have a motorway along the two diagonals *AC* and *BD* which required 56.6 miles of carriageway which they thought was the shortest solution. But they were wrong. There is a better solution. Can you find it?

60 Who nobbled the racehorse?

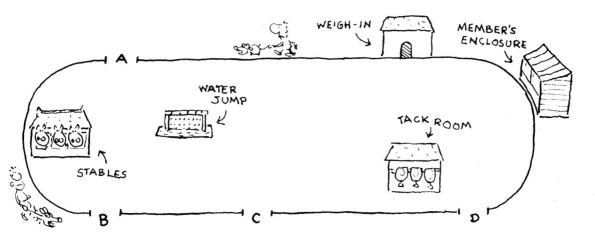

The favourite for the Winter Race Meeting at Aincot was stabled inside the racecourse on the night before the big race. Security inside the racecourse on that night was very tight with no one allowed inside the boundary fence from 11 p.m. until 7 a.m. the next morning. The guards and their dogs had had a cold night patrolling the grounds and at 7 a.m. when the four main gates were unlocked by the groundsmen and they were about to go home it began to snow. The snow delayed the arrival of the stable lad who entered at *B* and, before going to the stables to feed and exercise the favourite, had a few words in the tack room with the groom, who was there cleaning the saddle. He stayed with the horse right up to the start of the race, so imagine his distress when the horse ran very badly, finished last, and was shown to have been doped. He had his suspicions that one of the team of people surrounding the horse was guilty, so he set out to gather evidence about their movements between 7 a.m. and 7.15 a.m. when he had reached the stable. In this period of time he found that the owner of the horse had entered at *C* and strolled across to the member's enclosure. On the way the owner passed the trainer, who had entered at *D*, inspecting the water jump. The owner also saw the jockey on his way from *B* to the weigh-in, while the jockey passed the time of day with the groom, who had entered at *A*, when he was on his way to the tack room. They had all discussed the snow and remarked on their trails of footmarks which strangely didn't cross anywhere.

Who nobbled the horse?

61 Court card capers

Take all the Jacks, Queens, Kings and Aces from a pack of playing cards and arrange them in a 4 × 4 square array so that each row and each column contains exactly one card of each rank. One solution is shown but there are many more.

Now find a solution in which the diagonals as well as the rows and columns contain only one card of each rank.

But the real puzzle is to find a solution where there is only one card of each suit as well as only one card of each rank in every row, column and diagonal. There are 72 solutions ... take your pick!

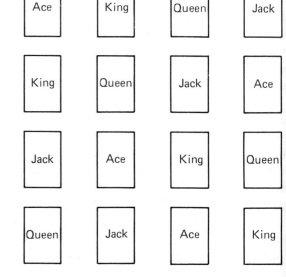

62 Heads and tails

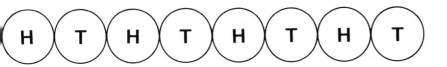

Take eight pennies and place them alternately
head and tail touching each other in a line as
shown. A move consists of moving two touching
pennies to one end or to a suitable space of the
row without changing their order.

Show that in four moves it is possible to
arrange them in the order T T T T H H H H
with the coins touching and in line.

63 The chapel hymnboard

The Methodist chapel at the village of Trepolpen
prided itself on its singing and everything was
done to ensure that it kept its good reputation.
At each service the organist's wife carefully
placed the number cards in the hymnboard so
that all the congregation could clearly see which
hymn was to be sung next.

But after many years' use the cards had
become very worn and a disgrace. The last straw
came at the Harvest Festival service when there
were not enough serviceable numbers left to
display the hymns chosen by the visiting minister,
and the organist threatened to resign.

The result was an emergency meeting of the
chapel trustees at which they agreed that they
would order a new set of cards. At first they
estimated that with 15 positions for numbers on
the board and 10 different digits possible they
would require 150 cards, which they couldn't
afford. However, the organist's wife pointed out
that in her experience a 6 could double as a 9
when placed upside down, and that different
numbers could be put on the two sides of a card.

61

She felt sure she could design a set of cards so that five of the 984 hymns in the Methodist hymnbook could be put up on the board with less than 100 cards.

What is the smallest number of cards which would fulfil all the requirements?

64 Find the radius of the circle

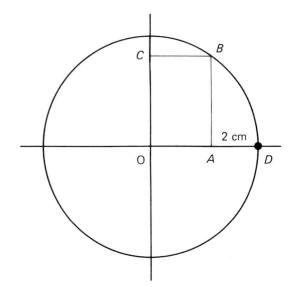

The rectangle *ABCO* has one vertex at *O*, the centre of a circle, and a second vertex *A* is 2 cm from the edge of the circle.

The vertex *A* is also a distance of 7 cm from *C*.

What is the radius of the circle?

65 As easy as ABC

Find *A*, *B* and *C* to make the adjoining addition sum correct.

$$
\begin{array}{r}
A\,B\,C \\
+\ A\,B\,C \\
A\,B\,C \\
\hline
B\,B\,B
\end{array}
$$

66 Fill the corners

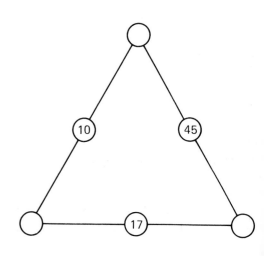

Find three numbers to put in the circles at the corners of this triangle so that the total of the numbers along each side is the same.

There are many solutions. How are they related to each other?

67 The end of the world!

A group of religious fanatics decided, after
intensive study of their holy books, and endless
use of a powerful modern computer, that the end
of the world would occur when the first day of a
century next fell on a Sunday.

How much longer do they give us?

68 How many will you take?

This is a game for two players. Start with a pile
of counters (matchsticks, coins or paperclips will
do).

Each player plays in turn and must remove
either 1 or 2 or 3 counters from the pile. The
player forced to remove the last counter loses the
game.

Play the game with your friends and see if you
can determine a winning strategy.

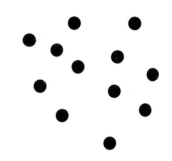

69 Envelopes of curves

'To envelope' the dictionary
tells us is 'to wrap up' or 'to
surround'. We use an
envelope to put a letter or
card in before sending it
through the post, and
mathematicians use the word
when they have a family of
lines (or other curves) which
surround a shape. In the
drawing the lines seem to
form a circle, although the
circle itself is not drawn, and
are said to be an envelope.

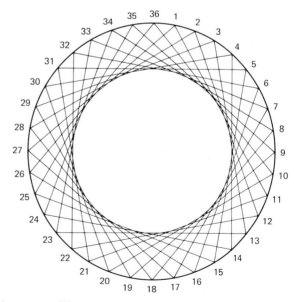

To draw this envelope and others in this activity you will
first need to draw a large circle (say 10 cm diameter) and
mark off 36 points on the circumference. This is easy with

a protractor, for the points will be at 10° intervals when measured from the centre of the circle.

The envelope of the circle shown above is then achieved by joining every point labelled n by a straight line to the point labelled $n + 10$. When $n + 10$ exceeds 36 just subtract 36 to find the correct point. For example, when $n = 29$, then $n + 10 = 39$ so take away 36 to leave 3.

Investigate the envelope obtained when straight lines are drawn from n to $n + 5$, n to $n + 15$, n to $n + 25$ etc.

More intriguing envelopes are obtained by using other rules to join the points.

The cardioid, meaning heart-shaped, is formed by joining 1 to 2, 2 to 4, 3 to 6, 4 to 8, 5 to 10, ..., n to $2n$.

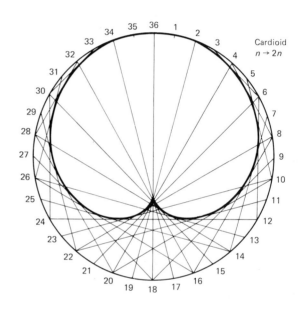

The nephroid, meaning kidney-shaped, is formed by joining 1 to 3, 2 to 6, 3 to 9, 4 to 12, 5 to 15, ..., n to $3n$.

Investigate the effect of using other rules.

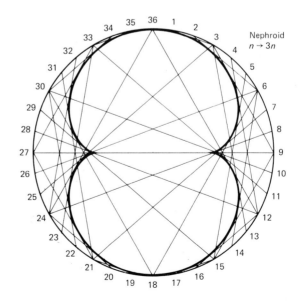

64

70 Four more ways to form an ellipse

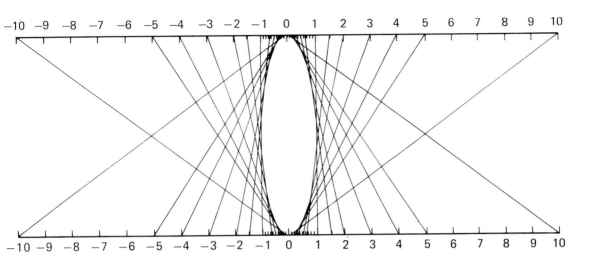

The first method of forming an ellipse, shown above, is by using the mapping of $x \to \frac{1}{x}$, that is the reciprocal function. Just draw two parallel lines and carefully mark off the numbers from -10 to 10 on each of them. Then draw in the lines which correspond to the mapping $x \to \frac{1}{x}$, such as $1 \to 1$, $2 \to 0.5$, $3 \to 0.33$, $4 \to 0.25$, $5 \to 0.2$, $10 \to 0.1$. The result is the envelope of an ellipse.

The further apart you draw the lines, the longer the ellipse. If you find the right spacing of the lines compared to the scale you use along the lines a circle will result. Investigate.

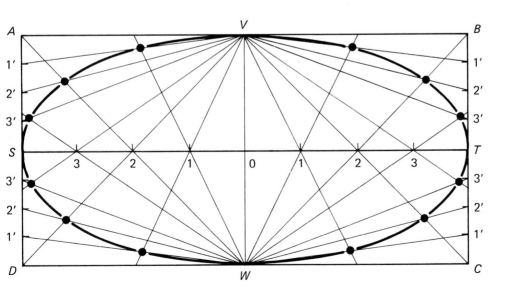

The second method is based on fitting an ellipse into a rectangle. Start by drawing a rectangle *ABCD* which is twice as long as it is wide, such as 16 cm by 8 cm. Then draw in the lines *ST* and *VW* which divide it symmetrically into four smaller rectangles as in the figure. Divide the line *ST* and the lines *AD* and *BC* into eight equal parts and label them as shown.

From *W* draw the line through the point labelled 1 on *OS* and from *V* draw the line to the point labelled 1′ on *AS*. Where they cross will be a point on the ellipse. Next draw the line from *W* through the point labelled 2 on *OS* and the line from *V* to the point labelled 2′ on *AS*. Again where they cross gives a point on the ellipse. Continue in this way and complete the lines for each quadrant then join up the points found by a smooth curve.

The ratio of the lengths of the sides of the rectangle, and the number of divisions mean too few lines and hence too few points to draw the ellipse accurately. But too many divisions only lead to confusion.

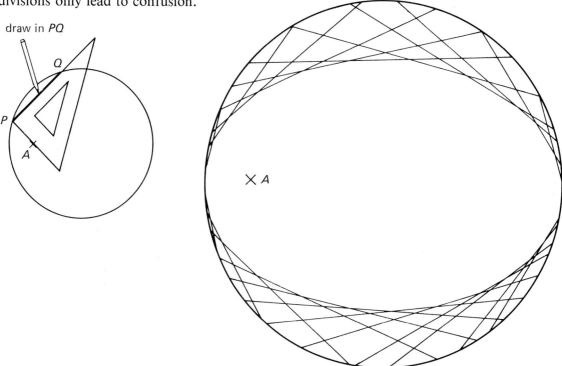

draw in *PQ*

For the third method you need a set-square. First draw a large circle (say 5 cm radius) and mark a point *A* towards the edge of the circle as shown in the diagram. Next place your set-square on the paper so that the right angle is on the circumference of the circle and one of the sides forming the right angle is just touching the point *A*. Now draw in the chord *PQ* of the circle corresponding to the other side of the right angle as shown. By moving the set-square to

many different positions, always touching A and with its
right angle on the circle, you will soon find the envelope of
an ellipse taking shape.

When you have formed one ellipse investigate what
happens with other positions for A.

A is one focus of the ellipse. Where is the other focus?

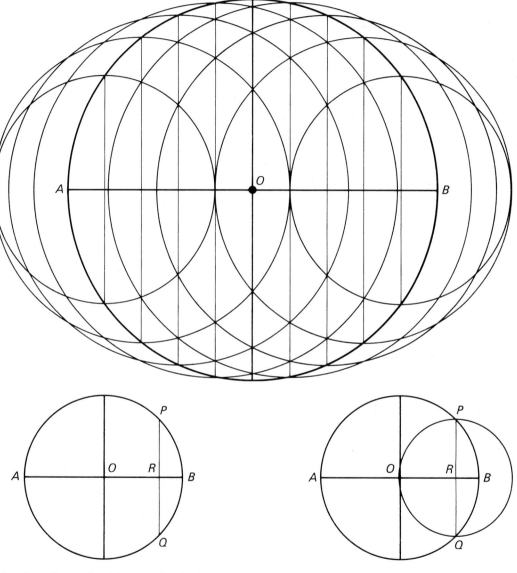

The fourth method interestingly forms an envelope of an
ellipse from circles. See the diagram. First draw a base
circle with a radius of, say, 5 cm. Draw in the diameter
AOB across the page and then draw in chords which are
perpendicular to this diameter at, say, 1 cm intervals. Now
take a chord such as PQ and draw the circle which has its
centre at R, the midpoint of PQ and which passes through
P and Q (i.e. PQ is the diameter of the circle).

Draw as many other circles based on the perpendicular chords as you wish to obtain a satisfactory envelope.

Notice that with this method some of the circles based on chords near to A and B lie wholly inside the ellipse so do not form part of its envelope.

71 Parabolas

When a cricketer hits a ball for six, or a child throws a stone through the air, the paths of the ball and stone follow curves which approximate to a parabola.

The shape taken up by the cables on a suspension bridge such as those across the rivers Tamar, Severn and Humber, or Brunel's famous bridge at Clifton across the river Avon are also parabolas.

But the parabolic curve is often found in the home as a reflector for an electric fire or the cross section of the reflector in a torch, where it has the ability to reflect, heat from the heating element or light from a bulb placed at its focus, in a narrow beam.

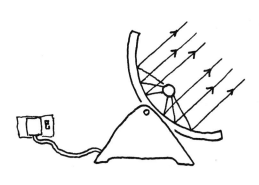

The same property is used to effect in:
rotating radar aerials of all sizes;
the large dish aerials such as those at Goonhilly which
beam and receive signals from artificial satellites;
the shape of the mirrors for optical telescopes and the
network of wires forming the aerial for radio telescopes.

After the straight line and the circle it is one of the most
commonly drawn curves at school because it is the shape of
$y = x^2$ or in fact any quadratic function, but here we look
at other ways of producing the curve.

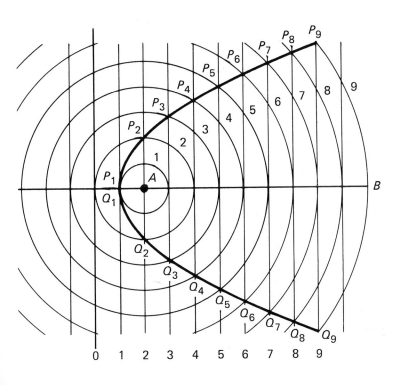

The first method of drawing a parabola, shown above, is to draw a set of circles with centre A and radii of 1 cm, 2 cm, 3 cm, 4 cm, ..., 9 cm. Then draw a set of parallel lines 1 cm apart touching the circles. Label the lines and circles up to 9 as shown, then carefully mark the points (indicated on the diagram with Ps and Qs) where the nth line crosses the nth circle. Join the points by a smooth curve. This is a parabola and the point A, at the centre of the circles, is its focus.

The focus has the unique property that if a light bulb is placed at the focus of a parabolic mirror then all the light is reflected parallel to AB, the axis of symmetry of the mirror. Conversely, any light travelling towards the mirror in the direction BA, will be reflected through the focus. It is this property which is used in telescopes, radar, searchlight reflectors and the like.

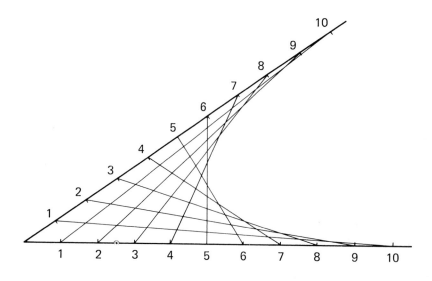

The second approach to forming a parabola shown here is the one much used by curve stitchers.

Draw two lines of equal length (say 10 cm), from a point, at an angle to one another. Mark off 10 equal divisions on each line then join the nth point on one line to the $(11-n)$th point on the other line, i.e. $10 \rightarrow 1$, $9 \rightarrow 2$, $8 \rightarrow 3$ etc.

No matter what the angle between the lines, the chords drawn produce an envelope for a parabola.

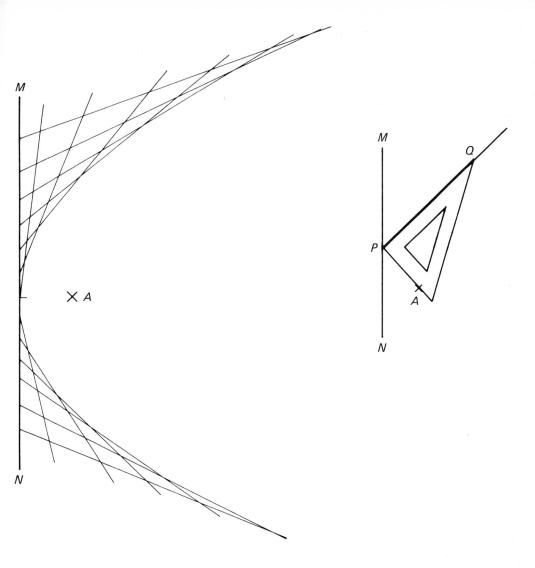

The third method again produces an envelope to the
parabola. Draw a line MN down the left-hand side of the
page and mark a point A, a short distance in from the
centre of the line as shown. Next place a set-square with its
right angle touching the line MN, and with one side
touching A. Now draw the line PQ along the other side of
the set-square forming the right angle. Move the set-square
to different positions always touching the point A and with
its right angle on the line, and draw in enough lines for the
envelope of the parabola to be clear.

The parabolic path is followed by many objects
projected under gravity. Follow the path of a stone which
has been thrown, the path of a shot when a shot putter
projects it into space, the path of a long jumper, . . ., the
path of a drop of water from a fountain. See what you can
observe.

72 The snowflake curves

Starting with an equilateral triangle, two interesting sequences of curves can be formed. See the diagram. To generate the snowflake sequence, first trisect each of the sides of the equilateral triangle and build smaller equilateral triangles on the centre third of each. Each new member of the sequence is then created by building yet smaller equilateral triangles onto the centre third of each straight portion of the last curve drawn.

The anti-snowflake curves are produced in a very similar way, but in that case the triangles which replace the centre third of each edge point inwards.

The easiest way to draw the curves is to start with isometric paper and let the initial equilateral triangle have a side of length 9 units.

If the length of the perimeter of the initial triangle is L units, explain why the lengths of the first two snowflake curves are $\frac{4}{3}L$ and $\left(\frac{4}{3}\right)^2 L$ respectively.

What are the lengths of the corresponding anti-snowflake curves?

What will be the lengths of the tenth curve in each sequence?

Investigate the areas inside the snowflake and anti-snowflake curves in terms of the area, A, of the initial triangle.

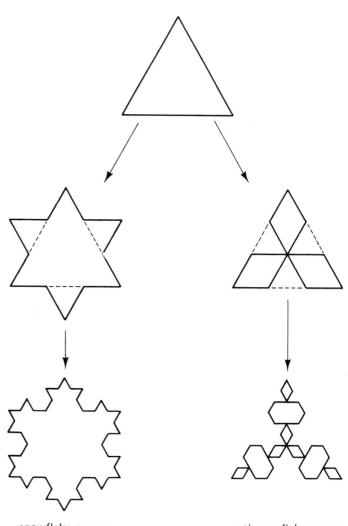

snowflake curves

anti-snowflake curves

73 The staircase paradox

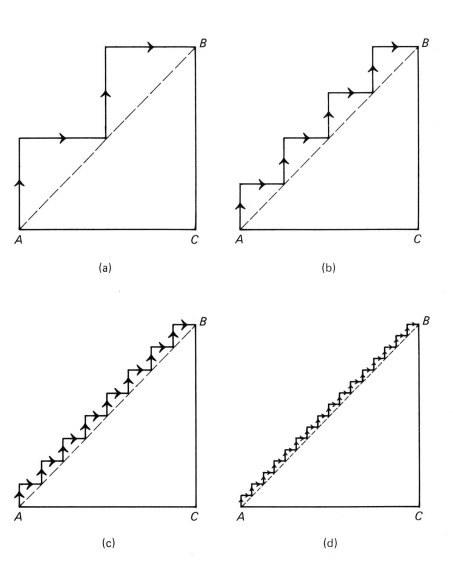

(a)

(b)

(c)

(d)

The family of curves being considered here are the
'staircases' from *A* to *B* where *ABC* is a right-angled
isosceles triangle. The first curve consists of two stairs and
the number of stairs doubles at each stage. If the length of
AC is 1 unit then it does not need much thought to see
that the length of each staircase is always 2 units.
However, by the tenth staircase in the sequence there will
be $2^{10} = 1024$ stairs and the curve will look very little
different from the hypotenuse *AB*. By the hundredth
staircase there will be more than
1 000 000 000 000 000 000 000 000 000 000 stairs and it will

be impossible to distinguish it from the line *AB*. But, by Pythagoras' theorem, the line *AB* is of length 2 units. Does this mean $\sqrt{2} = 2$?

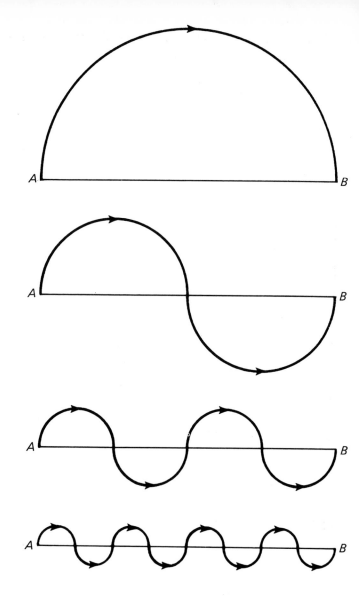

A similar paradox is produced by the sequence of curves formed from semicircles – the snake sequence.

If *AB* is of unit length show that each snake has a length of $\frac{1}{2}\pi$ units. Again, as the number of bends in the snake increases it will be indistinguishable from the line *AB* so is $\frac{1}{2}\pi = 1$?

74 Historical estimates for π

Historically mathematicians from varying civilisations have proposed estimates for π, the ratio of the circumference of a circle to its diameter.

The ancient Egyptians used 256/81 for this ratio, a fact recorded in the Rhind Papyrus, and a much better estimate than the Jews of Old Testament times who used the cruder approximation of 3 (see, for example, I Kings, chapter 7, verse 23). The ancient Greeks spent much thought on ways of improving their approximation of this ratio and Archimedes showed that its value lay somewhere between $3\frac{1}{7}$ and $3\frac{10}{71}$ by approximating to a circle by inscribed and circumscribed regular polygons.

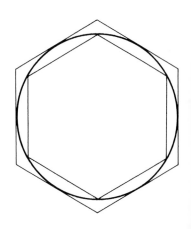

Hero of Alexandria also used $3\frac{1}{7}$ while Ptolemy believed the ratio to be equivalent to

$$3 + \frac{8}{60} + \frac{30}{3600}$$

influenced no doubt by the implied number base of 60 with which he was familiar.

Further interesting approximations by Asian mathematicians were

Baudhayana	$\frac{49}{16}$
Arya-Bhata	$\frac{62832}{20000}$
Brahmagupta	$\sqrt{10}$
Bhaskafa	$\frac{3927}{1250}$ and $\frac{754}{240}$

More recently Leonardo in the thirteenth century gave $\frac{1440}{458\frac{1}{2}}$ while in the sixteenth century Cusa thought the exact value was $\frac{3}{4}(\sqrt{3}+\sqrt{6})$.

These and many other famous mathematicians have had their names associated with estimates to π, although this symbol was only introduced in the eighteenth century when Euler and others saw the significance of π in analysis as well as geometry.

π is an irrational number which can never be expressed exactly by a decimal fraction although using modern computers it has been calculated to an accuracy of many thousand decimal places, the first 15 of which are

3.141 592 653 589 793

Use your calculator to compare the historical estimates with each other and place them in order of increasing accuracy.

A Chinese astronomer found an estimate of the form $\frac{abb}{cca}$ where a, b, c are different digits which is accurate to 7 significant figures. Can you find it?

75 What was the sum?

0.4482759

The result of dividing a 2-digit number by a 2-digit number with a calculator was as shown. What were the numbers?

76 Prelude to a marathon

```
  F I T
+ M E N
-------
  J O G
```

Each letter stands for one of the digits 1, 2, 3, ..., 9.
Each digit is used only once.

77 Dr Numerati's telephone number

Dr Numerati was one of those people who are forever spotting relations between numbers. She noticed, for example, that the number of her house and those of two friends formed three consecutive prime numbers whose product was equal to her telephone number.

Dr Numerati lived between her friends and had a five digit telephone number whose first digit was 6.

Find the number of Dr Numerati's house and of her telephone.

78 A magic diamond

Find the numbers to put in the circles so that the total along each line of the diamond is the same.

79 Palindromic dates

On 28 September a radio commentator drew attention to the interesting pattern of numbers in the date 28.9.82, when written in its usual abbreviated form. This set young Susan Nasus, the form swot, thinking about the distribution of such palindromic dates. She soon came to the conclusion that some years were richer in such dates than others and set herself the task of finding the two closest palindromic dates in this century. What do you make them?

80 The sponsored marathon

Instead of asking her sponsors for a fixed sum of money, say 3p, for each mile completed in the marathon, a runner struck on a clever idea to boost the proceeds for her chosen charity. She persuaded her sponsors that as each mile was progressively harder to run she would be happy if they gave her only 1p for the first mile, 2p for the second mile, 4p for the third mile and so on, doubling their sponsorship for each additional mile completed.

The argument sounded plausible but when the runner completed the marathon and called on her sponsors they were in for a nasty shock. What was it?

81 A calculator crossword

This crossword depends on the fact that many of the digits in a calculator display can look like letters when viewed upside down. Turn the book upside down and 'read' this number

35006

The clues for the crossword are given below in two forms, a calculation and a word form. Do the calculation, turn your calculator upside down and read off the word, then enter the word in the crossword. The word clue is there as a check and a guide to interpreting the 'word' in the display.

Calculation clue

Across

1. Enter 0.750
6. 638 + 266
7. 121 × 31
9. 1102 ÷ 29
10. 193 691 + 123 846
13. 4759 × 12
16. 2.347 − 1.794

Down

2. 32 867 + 44 478
3. 4466 ÷ 6380
4. 1769 × 20
5. 58 132 − 20 314
8. 67 × 5
11. 75 × 41
12. 3824 + 1947
14. 12 087 ÷ 237
15. 115 ÷ 230

Word clue

Across

1. Norwegian town
6. Found on a cooker
7. Small island
9. Exist
10. Boy's name
13. Water does this when heated
16. A competitor to 2 down

Down

2. Carried by snails
3. — and behold!
4. Very fat
5. Long standing best seller
8. What your eyes do for you!
11. Bitter fruit of the blackthorn
12. Need curing
14. This — Your Life!
15. Two thirds of an emergency

82 Variable based triangles

The essential property of a triangle is its rigidity and this is exploited time and time again in static structures such as in the timber framework of a roof.

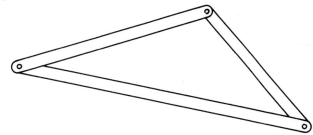

However an observant individual will also notice how the designer and the engineer have made use of triangle structures where one side of the triangle can vary in length. Several designs of car jacks make use of this idea. The one shown here consists of a four-bar linkage *ABCD* in the shape of a rhombus which is split into two triangles by a screw mechanism forming the diagonal *BD*. As the screw is turned clockwise the points *B* and *D* are pulled together thus shortening the base of the triangles *BCD* and *BAD* with the effect of increasing the height of both triangles and hence lifting the car.

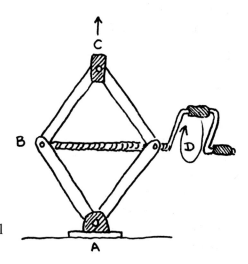

How does the height of *C* change with the change in length of *BD*? Investigate this with a car jack or a model made from geostrip or card.

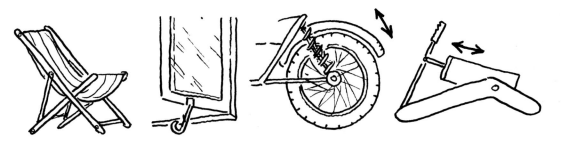

Often a variable based triangle is used to adjust the angle of a component such as a deck chair or a window fastening where one side of the triangle can be shortened or lengthened by so many holes or notches.

The suspension for the rear wheel of a motorcycle or the suspension of a car often incorporates a triangle where one side has been replaced by a spring which can respond to the bumps in the road. The usual design for a car foot pump also employs the same principle. When the brake pedal of a car is pressed it forms one side of a triangle, as with the foot pump and pushes a piston in a cylinder containing brake fluid whose pressure is transmitted along tubing to the brakes.

One mechanism whose use has become very widespread in recent years is that of the hydraulic ram in conjunction with a variable based triangle. The ram consists of a piston inside a cylinder filled with oil. The power from an engine is used to pump the oil from one side of the piston to the other thus pushing the piston along the cylinder and either shortening or lengthening the side of the triangle it forms.

Modern pumps can provide a considerable pressure difference across the piston so that the ram can exert a very large force when changing the shape of the triangle and this is exploited in the design of much of the machinery used by civil engineers for moving soil, by cranes, by agricultural machinery, by automated machines and robots in modern factories. The photos illustrate some uses. See what others you can find and make models from card to represent them.

83 Multiplying by three

Long before modern electronic computers were thought of engineers had devised many ways of mechanically multiplying a movement by a constant scale factor. This activity is an introduction to the idea of a constant multiplying factor in the design of mechanisms, and aims to encourage you to explore the concept further as a very tangible link between numbers and space.

Take first a system of two pulleys with diameters 12 cm and 4 cm connected by a belt. For every revolution of the 12 cm pulley the 4 cm pulley turns through three revolutions and the speed of the shaft connected to the small pulley, *B*, will always by three times the speed of the shaft connected to the large pulley, *A*.

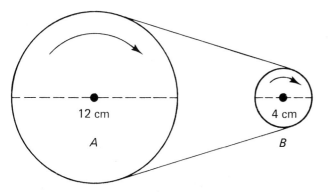

This kind of mechanism can be seen on some sewing machines and inside washing machines or on a lathe.

The sprockets and chain of a bicycle perform in much the same way. The chain wheel of a typical sports cycle has 42 teeth and one of the sprockets of the freewheel on a derailleur type gear, corresponding to a high gear, often has 14 teeth, so that the cycle's rear wheel will make three revolutions for every turn of the pedals. Without this simple mechanism a cyclist would have to pedal very quickly to progress even at a modest pace, or alternatively use very large wheels as with the early penny-farthing cycles.

Gear wheels are used similarly where a multiplying factor of three can be obtained by making the number of teeth on the first wheel three times the number on the second wheel. Have a look at an egg whisk or hand drill and count the number of teeth on the wheel to find the multiplying factor involved. A fishing reel is another good example of a

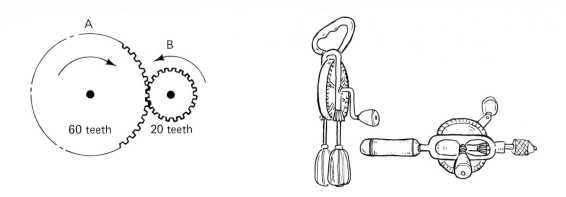

mechanism with a multiplying factor – from the number of turns on the winding drum to the number of turns made by the handle.

Linear motion can also be scaled up or down, and one way of doing this is to combine the mechanisms considered for rotation with winding drums. If the two pulleys discussed above are fixed to winding drums as shown in the diagram, then as the rope at A moves along its length a distance d, the rope at B will move along its length a distance $3d$, thus producing a multiplying factor of three for linear motion.

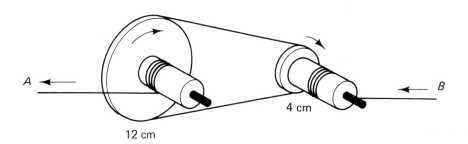

The same effect could be achieved using pulleys of equal size, but with the second winding drum having three times the diameter of the first, or, more simply, just having two winding drums of different diameters on the same shaft.

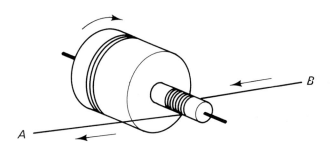

Pulley blocks are often used to produce a multiplying factor for linear motion. the diagram here shows one with a scale factor of three. As the rope at *A* is pulled down 1 metre, the three vertical parts of the rope around the two pulley blocks are each lengthened by a metre so the rope at *B* moves 3 metres along its length.

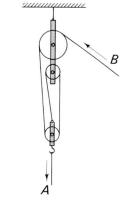

Levers too can easily be made to produce a scale factor of three and are widely used where only a limited movement is required such as in car hand brakes or clutch, brake and accelerator pedals. In both these diagrams, *B* moves three times as far as *A*.

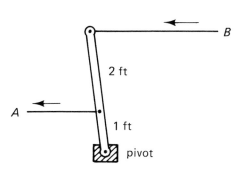

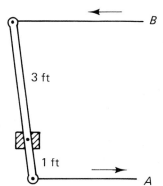

Much more widely used in recent years is the hydraulic ram. This is essentially a piston in a cylinder which is pushed along its length by a fluid. These hydraulic systems are to be found in most forms of transport from cars and lorries to jet airliners.

The diagram shows two pistons which slide in cylinders which are connected by a tube. The shaded area indicates the fluid in both cylinders and in the interconnecting tube. The fluid's volume remains constant, so that as piston *A* is pushed to the right the volume of fluid squeezed out enters the smaller cylinder and pushes piston *B* to the right. By making the cross-sectional area of piston *A* three times the cross-sectional area of piston *B* then the smaller piston will have to move three times as far as the larger piston for the decrease in the fluid in the large cylinder to balance the increase in fluid in the small one.

Another interesting way of mechanically producing a scale factor of three is to make use of a linkage of rhombuses not unlike part of the handle of lazy-tongs or the framework for a clothes airer (see the diagram). The linkage is fixed at *O,* and as *A* is moved away from *O* the three rhombuses all expand together with *O, A* and *B* in a straight line so that $OB = 3OA$.

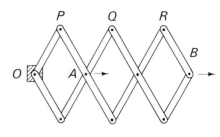

Use geostrip or strips of card and paper fasteners to make this linkage and investigate the paths of points such as *P, Q* and *R* as *A* travels on a straight line from *O.*

Investigate the design of other linkages which have a scale factor of three.

Lastly, one of the more primitive forms of mechanism, the wedge, can also be designed to have a multiplying factor of three. In the diagram two wedges are shown separated by rollers. The wedges have a slope of 1 in 3 so that for any change in height of *h* units there will be a horizontal movement of 3*h* units.

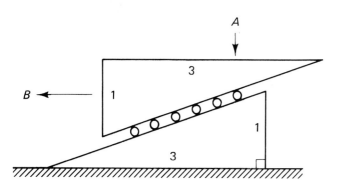

Investigate the multiplying factors involved in everyday mechanisms such as bicycles, sewing machines, clocks, lawnmowers, cars, drills etc.

Design a 'string factory' for a conjurer. This consists of a box which appears to double the length of string as it passes through the box.

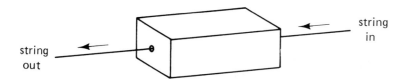

If you are clever you could arrange to have knots and/or coloured marks on the ingoing string whose distance apart is apparently doubled as the string emerges. To be most effective none of the mechanism should be visible, and the hole where the string comes out should be immediately opposite the hole where it goes in.

84 The hydrocarbons

The hydrocarbons are chemicals, such as petrol and paraffin, whose molecules are composed entirely of hydrogen and carbon atoms. In studying the ways in which carbon and hydrogen can combine, scientists have shown that they behave as if carbon atoms have four arms and hydrogen atoms only one arm each. To form a molecule, numbers of carbon atoms and hydrogen atoms group together 'holding hands' in such a way that no hand is left unheld.

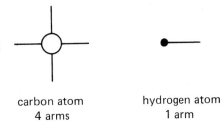

carbon atom
4 arms

hydrogen atom
1 arm

methane

ethane

propane

The simplest family of hydrocarbons, known as the alkanes, consists of single chains of carbon atoms surrounded by hydrogen atoms so that no atom holds more than one hand of another atom. The structure of the smallest three molecules in the alkane family are shown in the diagram. Their chemical formulae, which indicate the number of carbon atoms and hydrogen atoms in a molecule, are appropriately:

methane: CH_4 ethane: C_2H_6 propane: C_3H_8

The first three members of this family are all gases as is the next member, butane. Give its structure and deduce its chemical formula.

Octane, with a chain of eight carbon atoms in line, is a liquid, and a vital consitituent of petrol. What will be its chemical formula?

The alkanes with chains of more than 16 carbon atoms are all waxes and form the basis of wax candles. Give the chemical formulae for the alkanes having 17, 18, 19 and 20 carbon atoms respectively. Hence deduce a formula for the alkane with n carbon atoms in its chain.

Many hydrocarbons are formed by having branching chains of carbon atoms so that the variety of such molecules is enormous even when they apparently have the same chemical formula. For example, $C_{13}H_{28}$ can have over 800 significantly different structural forms. See if you can find the five different structures of molecules whose chemical formula is C_6H_{14}. One is already drawn to start you off.

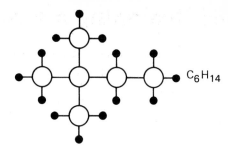

C_6H_{14}

With C_7H_{16} there appear to be nine different molecules possible. See if you can find them, but take care you don't count two as different when they are really the same; the arrangements of carbon atoms shown below may, at first, look different but they are holding hands with the same partners.

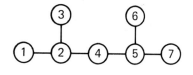

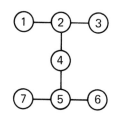

More complex molecules arise when a carbon atom is allowed to hold two, or even three, hands with another carbon atom. The gas ethene (C_2H_4) and the gas ethyne (C_2H_2) are examples of hydrocarbon molecules formed in this way.

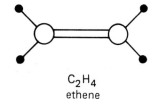

C_2H_4
ethene

When hydrocarbon molecules are not restricted to chains of carbon atoms, but rings of carbon atoms are allowed to form, the variety and complexity of the possible chemical compounds from carbon and hydrogen is astonishing. Two ring compounds are shown here to illustrate this.

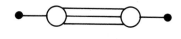

C_2H_2
ethyne

C_4H_8
cyclobutane

C_6H_6
benzene

Investigate all the different hydrocarbon molecules it may be possible for chemists to produce which contain four carbon atoms, and give their chemical formulae.

85 Designing a new dartboard

There seems to be no mathematical logic in the distribution of the numbers around a traditional dartboard. One way of overcoming this would be to redesign a board to maximise the sum of the differences between adjacent numbers round the board. Investigate!

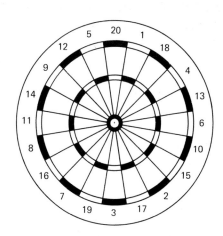

86 The car importer

A new assignment of Japanese cars had just been off-loaded from the freighter onto the dockside. The car importer checked that they were all of the same model as ordered, and went to complete the necessary paper work with the customs officials. While there, he was intrigued to notice that the total retail value of all the new cars was £1 111 111.

What was the retail price of the car (a whole number of pounds) and how many were there?

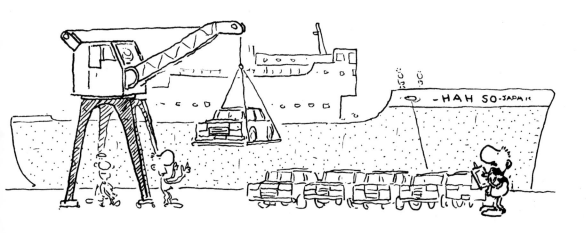

87 Look before you leap!

1   Which weighs heavier, a hundredweight of feathers or a hundredweight of coal?

2   How much earth is there in a hole in the ground which is 6 ft long, 2 ft wide and 6 ft deep?

3   A ship stood at anchor outside a port. To make access for visitors easier a rope ladder was hung over the side. The rungs of the ladder were 1 ft apart, and at 10 a.m., 12 rungs of the ladder were above the water. The tide was rising at a rate of 2 ft an hour, so the lady mayoress of the port delayed her visit to the ship until 1.00 p.m. by when, she argued, she would have fewer rungs to climb. How many rungs did she climb assuming that the tide continued to rise at the same rate, and that she arrived on time?

4   A squash racket and a ball together cost £12.80. The racket cost £12 more than the ball. What did the ball cost?

5   A farmer, who had been plagued by rabbits, went out early one evening armed with his shot gum. He found 13 rabbits feeding in his corn field and with his first shot killed one. How many rabbits remained in the field?

88 Find the digits

```
  A N T E
- E T N A
  ───────
  N E A T
```

There is a unique solution to this subtraction sum where each four-figure number has the same digits. Find it!

You might also like to find other examples of four letters which fit the same pattern and all form recognisable words.

89 The effect of inflation

The house which was first sold for £3500 when new in 1961 was sold in 1981 at a price of £34 000. The house has remained essentially unchanged in this period. What annual rate of inflation is this equivalent to, assuming that the rate remained unchanged?

In 1965 petrol cost 33p a gallon whilst in the summer of 1983 its price had risen to 184p a gallon. Does this represent a higher or a lower rate of inflation than that of the house price?

Assuming the same rates of inflation until the end of the century what will be the price of the house and of a gallon of petrol in the year 2000?

90 Octogenarian occupations

A retired octogenarian mathematics teacher playing around with a calculator given to him by his young teenage great granddaughter discovered that the difference between the cubes of the digits of his own age equalled the square of his great granddaughter's age. How old were they?

91 Prime factors

The following numbers appear very similar in form when written in base 10 but this can be deceptive. Use whatever means you have at your disposal to express them as a product of their prime factors.

$$11 =$$
$$111 =$$
$$1\ 111 =$$
$$11\ 111 =$$
$$111\ 111 =$$
$$1\ 111\ 111 =$$
$$11\ 111\ 111 =$$
$$111\ 111\ 111 =$$

92 Remove a rectangle

This is a game for two players. Start with a rectangular array of dots, for example a 5×7 array as shown.

A move consists of selecting a point in the array such as A and removing from the field of play all the points in the rectangle to the left and below the point.

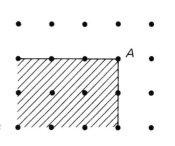

Players take turns to play and the loser is the person forced to select the last dot, which of course will always be at the top right hand corner.

A typical game is shown below where A plays first and choses points A_1, A_2, ... while B chooses B_1, B_2, ... and forces A to play the losing move.

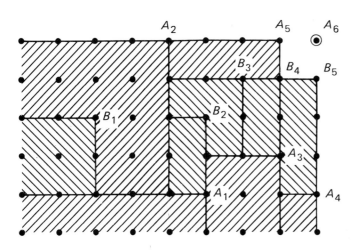

Can you develop a winning strategy?

93 Subtraction to addition

Learning to subtract two numbers, sooner or later leads to problems of borrowing or paying back. But it need not be the case. The method of complementary addition about to be described, ensures that whenever subtraction occurs, a digit is always taken from 9, so that no borrowing is called for.

Suppose, for example, we need to take 489 from 573 then we make life easy for ourselves by taking 489 from 999 instead, to give 510. Next we *add* 510 to 573 giving 1083, and finally we ignore the 1 in the thousands column, but add 1 to the units column to give a final answer of 84.

$$\begin{array}{r} 573 \\ - 489 \\ \hline \end{array} \quad \text{first} \quad \begin{array}{r} 999 \\ - 489 \\ \hline 510 \end{array} \quad \text{second} \quad \begin{array}{r} 573 \\ + 510 \\ \hline 1083 \end{array}$$

then finally $\cancel{1}083 + 1 = 84$

Here is another example to clarify the method:

$$\begin{array}{r} 35\ 274 \\ - 18\ 596 \\ \hline \end{array} \quad \text{first} \quad \begin{array}{r} 99\ 999 \\ - 18\ 596 \\ \hline 81\ 403 \end{array} \quad \text{second} \quad \begin{array}{r} 35\ 274 \\ + 81\ 403 \\ \hline 116\ 677 \end{array}$$

then finally $\cancel{1}16\ 677 + 1 = \underline{16\ 678}$

Check these subtractions using conventional methods or a calculator, then try out the method for yourself on sums of your own choosing.
Now explain why the method works.

94 A Russian two-step

In the past Russian peasants supposedly used a method of multiplication, which only required knowledge of the 2 times table. The method consisted of systematically halving one of the numbers being multiplied and doubling the other. Suppose, for example, we want to find the product of 39 and 79, then we proceed as follows:

$$39 \times 79 \qquad
\begin{array}{rrl}
39 & 79 & \leftarrow \\
\hline
19 & 158 & \leftarrow \\
9 & 316 & \leftarrow \\
4 & 632 & \\
2 & 1264 & \\
1 & 2528 & \leftarrow
\end{array}$$

Form two columns headed by 39 and 79. Divide the last number entered in the left-hand column by two and, ignoring any remainder, enter the result in this column. Now multiply the last number in the right-hand column by two and put the result in that column. Continue this

halving and doubling process until the last number in the
left column is 1.

Finally, add together all those numbers in the right-hand
column which come opposite an odd number in the left-
hand column (shown arrowed). The sum of these numbers
gives the required product.

$$39 \times 79 = 79 + 158 + 316 + 2528 = 3081$$

Try out this method for yourself on other numbers and
check the correctness of the product using a calculator or
other means.

Can you explain why the method works?

95 Magic squares revisited

Remembering an arrangement of the numbers 1 to 16
which form a magic square is not easy, but what follows
will give you a neat way of constructing one.

First fill in the numbers by counting along the rows in
order starting at the top left-hand corner as shown (a).

1	2	3	4
5	6	7	8
9	10	11	12
13	14	15	16

(a)

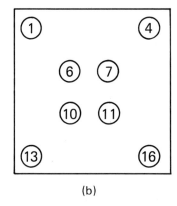

(b)

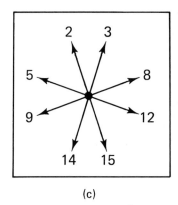

(c)

To be magic the numbers along each row, down each
column, and along the two main diagonals must each add
up to 34. A quick check shows that the diagonal elements,
shown ringed in (b), already satisfy this condition but the
row and column totals are incorrect. However, all that is
required to achieve a magic square is to interchange each
element not on the diagonals with the element diametrically
opposite to it, see (c). The resulting magic square is shown
in (d).

92

1	15	14	4
12	6	7	9
8	10	11	5
13	3	2	16

(d)

16	2	3	13
5	11	10	8
9	7	6	12
4	14	15	1

(e)

Alternatively, if the non-diagonal elements are left alone and each diagonal element is replaced by the element diametrically opposite to it a magic square again results (see (e)) which is a 180° rotation of the one already found.

The question now arises, can other 4×4 squares be generated in this way? One approach to investigate is to start putting the numbers 1 to 16 in a square in a regular way and seeing if transformations of the kind used above can convert it to a magic square. The example below gives one way which works.

1		2	
3		4	
5		6	
7		8	

$\rightarrow$

1	9	2	10
3	11	4	12
5	13	6	14
7	15	8	16

$\rightarrow$

1	8	15	10
14	11	4	5
12	13	6	3
7	2	9	16

(f)

Another way to generate further magic squares from a given magic square is to see if a permutation of the rows and/or columns can be found which will leave the totals along the diagonals equal to 34. Why will the totals of the rows and columns remain unchanged by such transformations?

Starting with the magic square (f) the following two magic squares have been obtained from it
(g) by interchanging the two middle rows
(h) by interchanging the first two rows and the second two rows.

1	8	15	10
12	13	6	3
14	11	4	5
7	2	9	16

(g)

14	11	4	5
1	8	15	10
7	2	9	16
12	13	6	3

(h)

Combining these transformations with each other, and with similar transformations for the columns many more magic squares can be found. See what you discover.

These transformations will not work with all 4×4 magic squares, for example the Nasik square, but with such squares other transformations are effective. With a Nasik magic square whose broken diagonals also sum to 34 new squares are found by 'rolling' the square up or down or sideways as if it were on a continuous band as shown below.

1	14	7	12
15	4	9	6
10	5	16	3
8	11	2	13

12	1	14	7
6	15	4	9
3	10	5	16
13	8	11	2

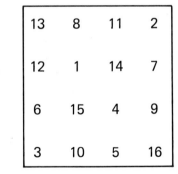

13	8	11	2
12	1	14	7
6	15	4	9
3	10	5	16

With these transformations alone the 1 digit can be moved to every position in the magic square. The Nasik square also remains magic when the first two rows (columns) and the second two rows (columns) are interchanged so many new squares can easily be generated. Investigate!

94

96 Do you know your birthday?

Perhaps you know on which day of the week you were born. You could hardly be expected to remember the day itself, and your parents may well have forgotten, although you, and they, will know your date of birth. So are you a Wednesday's child, full of woe, or a Monday's child fair of face, or what?

If you had the patience you could carefully count back the days through the years, not forgetting that every fourth year is a leap year, until you arrived at your birthday. That could take a long time. But don't despair, there is a much easier way as follows:

1 Let Y be the year you were born.
2 Let D be the day of the year you were born.
3 Calculate $X = (Y-1)/4$ and ignore the remainder.
4 Find $S = Y + D + X$
5 Divide S by 7 and note the remainder.

The day on which you were born can now be deduced by using the table below to see which day corresponds to the remainder.

Remainder	0	1	2	3	4	5	6
Birthday	Fri	Sat	Sun	Mon	Tue	Wed	Thur

The following worked example is based on my eldest daughter's birthday and should make the method clear. She was born on the 6th day of June in 1960.

1 $Y = 1960$

2 January   31 days
   February 29 days   as 1960 a leap year
   March   31 days
   April   30 days
   May   31 days
   June   6 days
   $D = 158$

3 $X = \dfrac{1960-1}{4} = \dfrac{1959}{4} = 489$ ignoring the remainder

4 $S = 1960 + 158 + 489 = 2607$

5 $2607 \div 7$ gives 372 remainder 3

Using the table, a remainder of 3 would indicate that my daughter was born on a Monday. That was a day I shall never forget as it was a Whitsun Bank Holiday Monday!

When you have found the days on which you and your family and friends were born see if you can see why the method works.

95

97 What scores are possible?

In a simplified version of darts the board had only two regions:

   an inner worth 11 points
   an outer worth 4 points

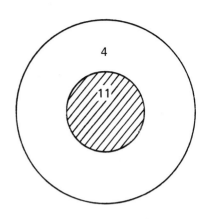

The players throw darts in turn and total their scores, with the winner the first person to achieve an agreed total.

When playing the game Katy and Helen noticed that no matter what they did they were unable to obtain some totals such as 21 so they sat down with paper and pencil and worked out all the unobtainable totals. Thankfully they found that, after a certain point, all totals were obtainable so agreed that, when they played in future, they would always make their target number large enough to be obtainable.

Find all the unobtainable totals in this case.

Investigate the pattern of unobtainable numbers when the inner and outer regions on the board take points values different from the above.

See if you can discover a formula which gives the largest unobtainable score when the inner is worth m points and the outer is worth n points.

98 The elusive digit

A certain calculator had a faulty circuit for its display, so that whenever the digit x ought to be displayed the digit y came up instead. The calculator, in all other respects behaved as it should. Using the calculator the following results were obtained

   $5672 + 7747 = 12\,975$
   $279 \times 767 = 87\,717$

where these were the numbers seen in the calculator display.

Which digit was wrongly displayed and by what digit was it replaced? What were the actual calculations above?

99 Chains of cube sums

Take any two-digit number which is divisible by 3, cube each digit and add the cubes together. Now cube the digits of your sum and repeat the process until something of significance occurs. For example,

$$36 \rightarrow 3^3 + 6^3 \qquad\qquad = 243$$
$$243 \rightarrow 2^3 + 4^3 + 3^3 \qquad = 99$$
$$99 \rightarrow 9^3 + 9^3 \qquad\qquad = 1458$$
$$1458 \rightarrow 1^3 + 4^3 + 5^3 + 8^3 \quad = 702$$
$$702 \rightarrow 7^3 + 2^3 \qquad\qquad = 351$$
$$351 \rightarrow 3^3 + 5^3 + 1^3 \qquad = 153$$
$$153 \rightarrow 1^3 + 5^3 + 3^3 \qquad = \text{\_}$$

What is the longest chain you can find before no new number is generated? Try to find a helpful way of recording your findings to avoid having to repeat calculations.

Now try the same process with numbers which are one less than a multiple of 3.

Numbers which are one more than a multiple of 3 have a different sort of end point when this process is carried out. See, for example, what happens when you start with 13.

Try investigating what happens with larger numbers as a starting point or using other powers than cubing.

100 Prime magic

Find prime numbers to put in the empty spaces to complete this magic square (i.e. the total of the numbers along each row, column and diagonal must be the same).

Investigate other 3×3 magic squares of prime numbers. Several exist where no number exceeds 300, but what is the smallest set of prime numbers which can be used?

1669		1249
	1039	

101 Surprise, surprise!

Write down any 3-digit number *abc* then repeat the digits
to form a 6-digit number *abcabc*.

Divide this number by 13 and ignore any remainder.
Divide your answer by 7 and ignore any remainder.
Finally divide by 11.
What do you notice? Explain the result.

102 Identical twins, quads and triplets

What must 49 be multiplied
by to produce 4949?

What must 38 be
multiplied to produce
383838?

Find four prime numbers
whose product with any
2-digit number *ab* will turn it
into the 6-digit number
ababab.

Investigate the effect on
2-digit numbers of the
product $73 \times 101 \times 137$.

103 Squares and cubes

There are many fascinating relations between sets of
numbers such as the Pythagorean triples (3, 4, 5) and
(5, 12, 13) whose squares satisfy

$$3^2 + 4^2 = 5^2 \qquad\qquad 5^2 + 12^2 = 13^2$$

and which relate to the lengths of the sides of right-angled
triangles. But not so well known are pairs of numbers
whose squares add up to a cube number. Such a pair are
47 and 52 for

$$47^2 + 52^2 = 17^3$$

Use your calculator to investigate other sets of numbers *a, b,* and *c* satisfying the relation

$$a^2 + b^2 = c^3$$

There are eight such sets where *a, b,* and *c* are all less than 50. Which of these has the further property that the sum of a^3 and b^3 is a square number?

By scrutinising your results you may spot a relation between the numbers which will enable you to generate readily as many further sets as you please.

104 Calculator golf

This is an estimation game which will take a while to set up but creates a lot of interest and worthwhile activity when played.

The game is played using a set of cards, each representing a hole of the golf course. On each card is a problem which amounts to estimating a number to a given degree of accuracy. The level of the problems is set in such a way that several estimates will probably be required to obtain the required accuracy, and the number of estimates a player needs will be his score for the hole. A 'hole in one' is always possible but very unlikely ... unless of course the problems set are too easy. An example of one of the cards, and what was recorded by Peter and Susan while playing it, is shown below.

Hole B
Find *b* given
$56.7 < b^2 < 57.7$
Par 4

Peter's record:

Hole *B* $56.7 < b^2 < 57.7$
$b_1 = 7.5$ $b_1^2 = 56.25$
$b_2 = 7.7$ $b_2^2 = 59.29$
$b_3 = 7.6$ $b_3^2 = 57.76$
$b_4 = 7.55$ $b_4^2 = 57.0025$

Score 4

Susan's record:

Hole *B* $56.7 < b^2 < 57.7$
$b_1 = 7.5$ $b_1^2 = 56.25$
$b_2 = 7.7$ $b_2^2 = 59.29$
$b_3 = 7.58$ $b_3^2 = 57.4564$

Score 3

Their first estimate suggests that they used their knowledge of multiplication tables to argue that as $7^2 = 49$ and $8^2 = 64$ then *b* must lie approximately halfway between 7 and 8, so they both gave 7.5 as their first estimate. Having used their calculator and found that $b_1^2 = 56.25$, and deduced that b_1 was too small, they tried $b_2 = 7.7$ for their second estimate only to find that $b_2^2 = 59.29$, and thus b_2 was too large. At this point they both appreciated that their estimates bracketed the value they wanted. But whereas Peter chose the number midway between them as his next estimate, Susan noticed that 7.5^2 was much nearer the hole than 7.7^2 and, allowing for this, holed with her next estimate.

Peter's use of the mid-point of his estimates at each stage will always give him a reasonable score, but Susan's more thoughful approach will win more holes!

Some more examples are given below

Hole D

Find d given

$$181 < 17 \times d < 183$$

Par 3

Hole H

Find h given

$$4.5 < \frac{269}{h} < 4.9$$

Par 4

Hole M

Find m given

$$128 < m(m+9) < 130$$

Par 4

Hole Y

Find y given

$$0.90 < \frac{y-10}{y+10} < 0.91$$

Par 5

When a good selection of cards has been made up, then a variety of 'courses' can easily be created.

105 Fox and geese

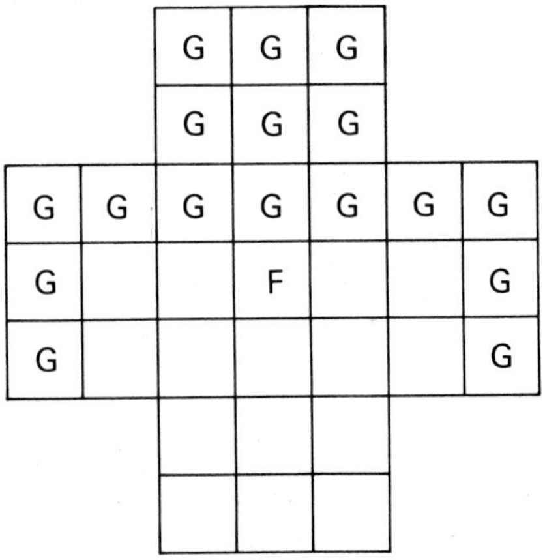

This is a game for two players played on a squared board in the shape of a cross as shown. You will need 17 counters to represent the geese and these are placed in the squares marked G in the diagram. One more counter of a different colour or size can then be used for the fox who starts at the square marked F, in the centre.

The geese can move one square at a time either left, right or down but not up or diagonally.

The fox can move one cell at a time either left, right, up or down. Further it can jump over a goose (and remove it), if the goose is in its path and the square on the other side of the goose is vacant.

The object of the game is for the geese to surround the fox so that it cannot move, while the fox tries to consume the geese and avoid capture.

The geese have the first move.

Play the game and see if you can devise a winning strategy.

106 All present

Generating numbers which contain all the digits 1, 2, 3, ..., 9 once only has fascinated many people. Unfortunately most calculators can only display 8 digits, so more than pressing keys will be required in any investigation of such numbers.

Complete the following:

$11\ 826^2 =$ $19\ 377^2 =$

$12\ 543^2 =$ $19\ 629^2 =$

$15\ 681^2 =$ $23\ 178^2 =$

$18\ 072^2 =$ $29\ 034^2 =$

There are in fact 83 square numbers which contain all the digits 1, 2, 3, ..., 9 only once. If you have access to a computer you might try programming it to find them.

Now try the following:

$$11\ 113^2 - 200^2 \quad =$$
$$31\ 111^2 - 200^2 \quad =$$
$$11\ 115^2 - 294^2 \quad =$$
$$191\ 161^2 - 188\ 560^2 =$$

There are 362 880 different possible numbers which can be formed using the digits 1, 2, 3, ... 9 once only. How many of them are prime?

101

107 Postage due

At the end of the day a secretary was faced with putting stamps on a large number of packages. She had plenty of stamps but they were only in two denominations and she was not sure that she would always be able to find the right combination to match the postage due. However, experience showed her that although she could not find a combination of the stamps to make 39p, any higher postage due could be arranged with a suitable combination of the stamps available.

Assuming that the stamp denominations were a whole number of pence, what were they?

108 Ann's tower

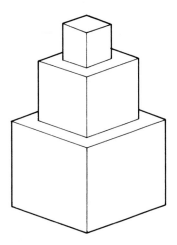

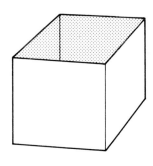

One of Ann's Christmas presents was a box of building bricks. The bricks were all cubes with an edge of 5 cm and completely filled the box which was also in the shape of a cube. Like many young children Ann was fascinated with building towers and it wasn't long before she had tipped out all the bricks and started building. She started by building a large cube, then a smaller cube on top of that and a yet smaller cube on top of the latter. When the three cubes were complete she could still look over the top of her tower when standing, which disappointed her, but she had the satisfaction that she had used every single brick in her construction.
  How high was the tower?

109 Reconstructing the manor house

Some historians were trying to piece together evidence, from a variety of sources, on an old manor house, long since destroyed. They knew that one of the main rooms had a long wall completely oak panelled, while its end wall opposite the doorway was covered by a tapestry purchased in France. The floor had been covered by a specially made Persian carpet. Many details of the design and colours were known in each case, and they knew the areas of the panelling, the tapestry and the carpet were 648 ft², 388 ft² and 1296². Nowhere, however, could they find any reference to the linear dimensions of the room. Can you help them?

110 The blanket box

Peter went to a DIY shop to buy some plywood to make a rectangular box in which to store blankets. The shop had a policy of charging at a high rate for cutting into a new sheet of plywood, but at a low rate for offcuts. Peter searched diligently among the stack of offcuts and eventually found three pieces which exactly fulfilled his requirements. One piece was just right for the bottom and a side. Another piece, when cut in two, would make a side and an end. The third piece was just right for the top and the remaining end. The DIY owner worked out the areas of the three pieces (in order to compute their cost) as

6048 cm²   4563 cm²   and 4995 cm²

Ignoring the thickness of the wood involved, what are the dimensions of the box?

111 Three in a line

This is a noughts and crosses type game, which can be designed to give practice in different arithmetic operations at the level required.

The example shown here is of a 4×4 array of numbers formed from the sixteen possible products of a number from $A = \{23, 41, 19, 36\}$ and a number from $B = \{17, 28, 35, 12\}$. They are not filled in on a regular pattern as with a conventional multiplication table, but consciously jumbled up!

644	391	665	228
1148	276	805	492
323	612	697	532
1435	432	1008	1260

Two players take turns to play. A player's turn consists of choosing a number from A and a number from B, and the opponent uses a calculator to find their product. The player can then mark the appropriate square. The first player to mark three squares in a straight line wins.

To save writing out all the numbers the game can be played in a blank 4×4 square with players marking the squares they have singled out with their choice of numbers using a O or X or their initials.

112 Topsy-turvy

Investigate the set of numbers which have the property that when they are multiplied by nine their digits are reversed.

When you have found the underlying pattern to that set of numbers try finding the numbers whose digits are reversed when multiplied by four.

113 Divisibility

Can you arrange the digits 1, 2, 3, 4, 5, 6, 7, 8, 9 in an order so that:

the number formed by the first two digits is divisible by 2
the number formed by the first three digits is divisible by 3
the number formed by the first four digits is divisible by 4
and so on up to nine digits?

The order 1 2 3 6 5 4 9 8 7 looks promising as

        1 2 is divisible by 2
       1 2 3 is divisible by 3
     1 2 3 6 is divisible by 4
   1 2 3 6 5 is divisible by 5
1 2 3 6 5 4 is divisible by 6

Unfortunately 1 2 3 6 5 4 9 is not divisible by 7. Back to the drawing board and try again!

114 Calculator challenges

1 The square number 25 has the property that when its digits are increased by 1 it is converted to 36, another square number. There is just one 4-digit square number with the same property. What is it?

2 A 2-digit number ab has the property that its square differs from the square of ba by a square number. What are the numbers?

3 The product of the sum of two square numbers with the sum of two square numbers is always the sum of two square numbers. For example,

$$(1^2 + 2^2)(2^2 + 3^2) = 65 = 4^2 + 7^2.$$

Investigate this statement.

115 The Giant and the Dwarfs

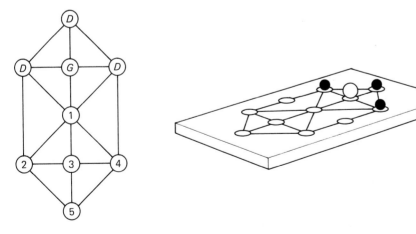

This is a game for two players. The board shown above can easily be drawn on a piece of paper, but a more permanent version could be made by drilling holes in a block of wood and using coloured pegs for pieces, or making hollow depressions for the circles and using marbles as pieces.

Three counters are required for the three dwarfs (D) and a counter of a different colour or size is required for the giant (G). The starting position is shown above. One of the dwarfs moves first and they can move down or across to any adjacent cell which is not already occupied. Thus for example in the opening move the left-hand dwarf could move straight down to circle 2, or diagonally to circle 1. The giant can move in a similar way but it is also allowed to move up the board.

The object of the game is for the dwarfs to surround the giant so that it cannot move.

Play the game and see if you can devise a winning strategy.

What would happen if you tried a different starting position for the pieces?

116 Rhyme around

Sir, I bear a rhyme excelling
In mystic force and magic spelling
Celestial sprites elucidate
All my own striving can't relate.

See, I have a rhyme assisting
My feeble brain, its tasks ofttimes resisting.

Both these rhymes were composed for the same purpose. What was that purpose?

117 The Ruby wedding

At their Ruby wedding celebrations William and Ruth had all their family to a party. Reflecting on their long life together William recalled how he had first fallen in love with 'young Ruth' when they had shared a desk at school together many years ago. Looking around at his children and their families he wondered whether they would all be together for a golden wedding anniversary and, so speculating, he realised that the difference between the square of his age and the square of his wife's age was exactly equal to the square of the number of their children.

How old were William and Ruth when they married, and how many children did they have?

118 The medieval courtyard

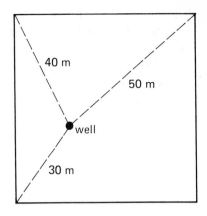

A medieval monastery was built around a courtyard in the form of a square. In the courtyard was the well from which the monks obtained all their drinking water. The well was so placed that its distance from three consecutive corners was 30m, 40m and 50m respectively.

How big was the courtyard?

119 Fill the gaps

In each of the following sequences of numbers find a rule to fill in the gaps and then give the next number in each sequence

(a) 1, − , 7, − , − , 16
(b) 1, − , − , 7, − , 16
(c) 1, − , − , − , 7, 16

What other rules can you find for filling in four gaps between 1 and 16?

120 Find the route

It is possible to start at the top left hand corner, move one square to a 1, then move two squares to a 2, then move three squares to a 3, and so on, without revisiting any square, and ending with the 8 in the bottom right hand corner.

Moves can be made only vertically and horizontally not diagonally.

See if you can find such a route.

Start	1	3	2	5	4	4	6
2	4	5	3	4	6	7	4
5	2	3	5	3	5	6	5
4	3	6	3	5	4	7	4
3	4	7	6	5	7	6	5
5	6	5	3	7	6	4	7
4	7	4	5	6	5	5	7
6	5	7	7	5	6	4	(8)

121 501 up!

With the evergrowing popularity of darts a group of
players decided to make the game of '501 up' more testing
for themselves by only allowing a turn to count if the total
score for that turn was a prime number.

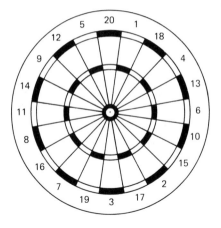

You need to know that a player throws three darts in a
turn, and each dart can score 1, 2, 3, ..., 20, or double or
treble any of these numbers. Also a dart can score 25 by
entering the 'inner' ring, or 50 for a bullseye. A dart could
also score 0 by missing the board, or not sticking in the
board and falling to the floor.

Thus, for example, a turn in which the three darts ended
up in a treble 20, a double 12, and a 5, would give a total
score of 89, a prime number, and so be counted. However
three darts each scoring a treble 20 with a total score of
180 would not count.

What are the three highest scores obtainable for a turn
which would be countable?

What is the smallest number of turns in which it would
be possible to reach a total of 501?

If the game has to end with a 'double' what is the
smallest number of darts a player could throw to win.

An alternative version of the game was devised which
only allowed a turn to count if the running total when
counting back from 501 was a prime number. (In this case
the total score for each turn need not be prime.)

Show that zero can be reached throwing a double with
the ninth dart.

122 One, two, three, four, five ...

Alan, Betty and Carol made up a game to challenge each
other's ingenuity with a calculator. The object of the game
was to find the most efficient way of obtaining each of the
integers 1 to 20, in turn, in their calculator display. This
was not as easy as it sounds, for they only allowed
themselves to press the digit keys in numerical order,
without repetition, starting with 1 each time. Thus for
example, when 3 had been entered, the next digit key
pressed must be 4.

While playing this game, to obtain 8:

Alan used $-1+2+3+4=$

while Betty used $1 \times 2 \boxed{x^y} 3 =$

and Carol used $.1 \boxed{1/x} - 2 =$

A point was scored by the person who had used the fewest key presses for a given number or, in the case of a tie, the person who had entered the smallest number of digits. In the above game Alan used 9 key presses while Betty and Carol each used only 6. Carol gets the point however as she had only used the digits 1 and 2.

123 Crossed ladders

In an alleyway between two houses two ladders are leaning against the walls as shown.

AB is 8 m long
CD is 10 m long

The ladders cross at a height of 4 m above the ground. How far apart are the houses?

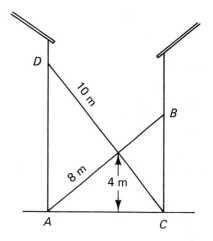

124 Target

This is a calculator game to encourage creativity and test ingenuity.

At the start of the game two pieces of information are given:

1 the keys which are allowed to be pressed,
2 a target number.

Ideally the first kind of information could be on a pack of cards which are chosen in turn or selected at random, while the target number could be generated, say, by entering any number into a calculator, pressing the $\boxed{\sqrt{}}$ key twice and using the last two digits in the display.

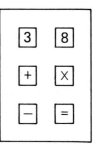

Suppose a card allowed the use of the keys for 3, 8, +, ×, − and =, and the target number was 80. The object of the game is to obtain the target number in the calculator display with the smallest number of key presses.

For example

| 8 | × | 3 | × | 3 | + | 8 | = |

| 8 | × | 8 | + | 8 | + | 8 | = |

both give 80 in 8 key presses, but by far the shortest is

| 8 | 8 | − | 8 | = |

with only 5 key presses.

Scoring can be on the basis of 1 point for the player with the 'shortest' method or, perhaps better, a point for each different method found.

125 One and zeros

Given that the only digit keys you are permitted to use on your calculator are the 0 and the 1 it is an interesting activity to see in what different ways other numbers can be obtained in the calculator display.

For example, 120 can be obtained by

| 1 | 1 | × | 1 | 0 | + | 1 | 0 | = |

or | 1 | 1 | × | = | − | 1 | = |

or | 1 | 1 | 0 | + | 1 | 0 | = |

The first way here required nine key presses whilst the other two only require seven key presses so could be said to be more efficient.

See if you can find the most efficient way with your calculator of obtaining the following

    (a)   77   (b)   979   (c)   1432
    (d) 1958   (e) 2046   (f)   15 983

126 A cautionary tale

To give his class practice in using calculators a mathematics teacher set them to solve the simultaneous equations

$$32.26x + 14.95y = 28.35$$
$$187.3x + 79.43y = 83.29$$

He hadn't worked out the solution himself because he had taken the question from a textbook for which he had the answers. Unfortunately he had misread one of the coefficients and given the class 14.95 where the book had 14.96. He realised his mistake well into the lesson, but argued with himself that such a small change could hardly affect the answer. Only when the children's work came in and the brightest girls had answers which agreed with each other but looked very different from those in his book did he work out both sets of solutions for himself. What did he find? Was the book wrong? Were the girls wrong? Could both be right? Investigate and try to account for your findings.

127 Another calculator crossword

The clues are given below in two forms, a calculation and a word form. Use one to check the other and put the words into the crossword blank.

Across	Calculation clue	Word clue
1	$3175 + 4539$	Small mountain
3	$6335 \div 7$	Cry
6	39×17	'Go to work on an ...'
7	357×89	Girl's name
9	$4642 - 891$	Singular of 8 down
13	$2898 + 675$	Otherwise
14	$760 \div 19$	Exclamation
16	$4492 - 685$	Fleshy part of ear
17	21×1667	Not tight

Down		
1	$45\ 552 \div 13$	Found in the garden
2	$635\ 499 - 317\ 692$	Boy's name
3	5×923	Utter long audible breath
4	$3456 + 2052$	In charge at work
5	$58\ 316 - 982$	Parts of feet
8	$10\ 588\ 947 \div 197$	Scilly ...
10	$419 + 314$	Snake-like fish
11	42×43	Mongolian Desert
12	$1527 - 817$	Liquid which floats on water
15	$918 \div 27$	Not she

Now make a list of all the words you can find using the letters which can be produced in your calculator display and then create your own calculator crosswords.

112

COMMENTARY

5 The car jam

Take the width of a car as 1 unit, its length as 2 units, and
L, R, U, D to mean left, right, up, down respectively.

Then car 1 will be released by the following car moves:
3(L1), 4(U1), 5(R2), 11(U2), 6(U1), 7(U2), 12(L4), 8(L1),
13(U1), 10(R1), 1(D6). The key to the solution is to
appreciate that 10 must move to the right which can only
be achieved by moving 13 up, which in turn requires that
12 moves left etc.

Try making similar puzzles of your own.

6 The flight controller's nightmare

No solution is possible.

As soon as flight paths have been arranged from A and
B to P, Q and R then one of these airports (P in the
diagram) will be inaccessible to flights from C. Eight of the
nine flight paths can be planned but not the ninth.

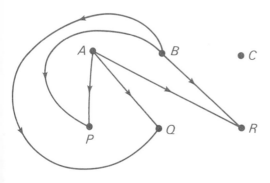

7 The vanishing act

Your eyes don't deceive you, there are only eleven lines
after you have slid the paper along. However the lines have
all grown slightly in length. The original total length of the
twelve lines together was $12 \times 3 = 36$ cm.

The length of the new lines is 36 cm $\div$ 11 $= 3\frac{3}{11}$ cm.

Measure with your ruler to see the increase in length.

If you had started with 25 lines of length 3 cm, and say
1 cm apart, then this process would have led to 24 lines of
length $3\frac{1}{8}$ cm.

Investigate.

8 Mystifying matchsticks

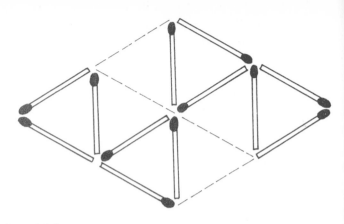

A very satisfying solution when you have found it!

9 Calculator cricket

Experience shows that this game is enjoyed by a wide range of participants, with test matches between England and Australia ever popular.

It not only improves the estimating skills of the players bowling but also that of the players batting who are trying to set sums which they think will be difficult to estimate and do their own estimating in the process!

In another version of the game the allowable sums will be on a pack of cards and the batsman will draw eleven cards from the pack in turn. Packs could be produced for different ability levels so that a player of low ability could be matched against a player of a higher ability and have a good chance of winning.

Alternatively two or more players could all estimate answers to the same set of sums and the winner would then be the one with the lowest aggregate of differences.

10 Generating straight-line motion

Making up linkages and manipulating them gives spatial experience. This activity is essentially a model-making one but can be linked with industrial archaeology and visits to places such as the Science Museum, South Kensington, or any of the many fascinating museums and sites around the country concerned with the industrial revolution such as the Ironbridge Museums or the Kew beam engines. The mechanisms concerned with the woollen industry contain many fascinating examples of engineering ingenuity which are all concerned with spatial appreciation.

The mechanisms described in this activity make interesting wall displays which children can, and will, manipulate and in so doing gain a better understanding of geometry.

An excellent book on linkages, if it can be found in a library, is *Geometrical Tools* by R C Yates, published in America in 1949. *Mathematical Models* by Cundy and Rollett also has a section on linkages for linear motion.

11 Make a mobile to defy gravity

It is a valuable experience to make this and similar mobiles, both from the understanding it brings to the link between parallelograms and cross-over quadrilaterals, as well as the understanding the 'weighting' process brings to the moments of forces. Apart from which it is a very pleasing mobile to observe when complete and hung from the ceiling.

12 The triangular building site

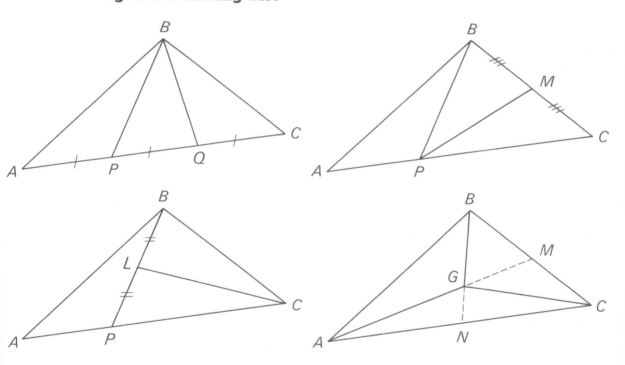

This is a creative activity based on areas of triangles. In the four solutions shown here P and Q trisect AC while L, M, N are the mid-points of BP, BC and AC respectively. G is the centroid of the triangle and gives the mathematically most satisfying solution. However, if all the sites are to have a frontage on the main road then the first solution is best.

13 Ring the triangle

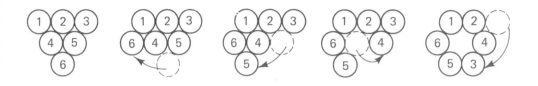

14 K9 or One man and his dog

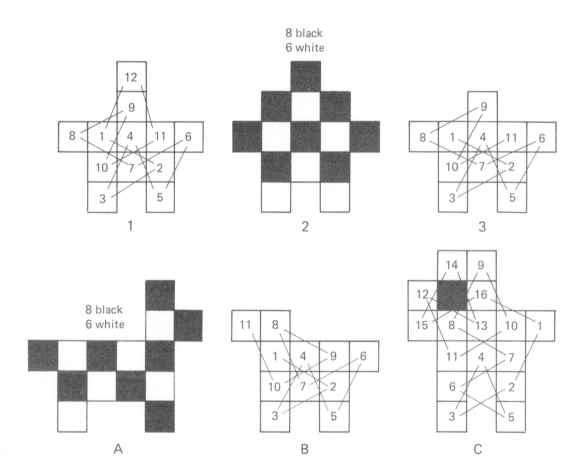

1 pairs with C, 2 pairs with A, 3 pairs with B.

The key to these is to shade the squares alternately black
and white as on a chessboard, and then to consider the fact
that a knight must always move to a square of a different

colour. From this consideration alone it can be seen that the second man and first dog, which have an imbalance of 2 between their black and white squares, could not be traversed by a knight without re-visiting a square en route. The first man and the third dog have no imbalance between their numbers of black and white squares, a necessary condition for a re-entrant tour, and a re-entrant tour on each is shown in the diagram above. The remaining man and dog have an imbalance of 1 between their black and white squares which means that any tour will always end on a square of the same colour as the starting square and thus a re-entrant tour would not be possible.

Investigate other shapes on which it is possible to trace knight's tours.

15 The anti-litter campaign

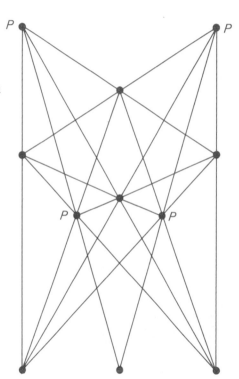

11 bins are required to ensure 3 on each path. The solution is indicated by the small circles which occur at all the 10 points where four paths intersect, and where two paths intersect at the middle of the bottom end of the park.

Only four park attendants would be required to ensure the presence of at least one on each path and their placing is indicated by the letter P on the diagram.

This puzzle is best tackled by making a drawing of the plan of the paths and experimenting with positioning counters at intersections to aid one's thinking.

16 The railcar terminus

The solution to this puzzle depends on appreciating that the effect of driving a set of railcars around the loop is that they re-enter the main line in the opposite order to that which they left it. To put railcar 7 in the position to depart first requires, initially, that it is positioned on the left hand end of the line of railcars, by driving 1, 2, . . . 7 around the loop, and then to drive all nine railcars around the loop.

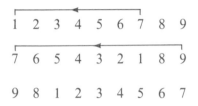

9 8 1 2 3 4 5 6 7

These two moves correctly position railcar 7 which can now be left alone and the next railcar to depart, number 9 be repositioned. The strategy would be to first get railcar 9 to the left hand end and then reverse the order of the eight railcars to the left of railcar 7 to achieve the correct position of railcar 9. In this case railcar 9 is already conveniently at the left hand end so only one move is required and when it is carried out it also carries railcars 8, 1 and 2 into their correct departure positions.

9 8 1 2 3 4 5 6 7

6 5 4 3 2 1 8 9 7

The next railcar to position is thus number 4 and this requires two moves

6 5 4 3 2 1 8 9 7

4 5 6 3 2 1 8 9 7

3 6 5 4 2 1 8 9 7

Again the moves conveniently also place railcar 5 in the right departure position so it only remains to interchange railcars 3 and 6 to achieve the required order

3 6 5 4 2 1 8 9 7

6 3 5 4 2 1 8 9 7

In this case the correct departure order has been achieved by 6 moves, where a move is defined as taking a set of railcars around the loop.

How many moves would be required to change the railcars so that they can depart in the order

3 1 5 9 6 4 7 2 8 ?

What would be the worst departure order the controller would have to deal with?

17 Paving the patio

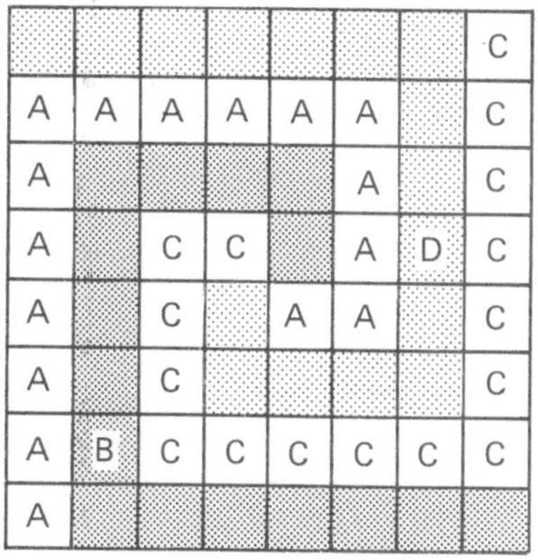

							C
A	A	A	A	A	A		C
A					A		C
A		C	C		A	D	C
A		C		A	A		C
A		C					C
A	B	C	C	C	C	C	C
A							

18 Make a twistable tetrahedral torus

The rings of tetrahedrons described here are examples of a whole family of such rings first discovered by J M Andrews and R M Stalker.

The ring of six tetrahedrons has been shown here with isosceles triangles for faces, as that formed from equilateral triangles has restricted mobility. However all the rings with eight or more tetrahedrons can be rotated when the tetrahedrons are regular. By studying the nets it should be clear how rings can be produced with as many tetrahedrons as you wish.

There is further discussion of these rings in *Mathematical Recreations and Essays* by Rouse Ball. You may also find nets to cut out for some of these rings in the very attractive series of booklets by Tarquin Publications such as *Make Shapes*. *M. C. Escher Kaleidocycles* by Schattschneider and Walker contains seventeen easy to assemble models of rings of tetrahedrons delightfully decorated in colour with Escher designs.

20 Spot the pattern

The colour of a circle is determined by the two circles immediately above and left and right of it. If the two upper circles are the same colour, then the lower circle is white, if different the lower circle is black.

Each row of circles is to be thought of as a continuous band so that the circle at the right hand end is followed by (or next to) the circle at the left hand end.

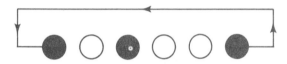

Thus in deciding the colour of the last circle in a new row, it has to be seen as below the first and last circles of the previous row. After the first row the number of black circles (and of white circles) must be even. Why?

An all white row can only follow from an all white row or an all black row. So it depends on the possibility of an all black row. Now an all black row can only be obtained from a row which alternates white and black and this can be shown to be unobtainable as the following argument shows.

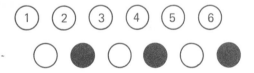

Suppose 6 is white, then 1 must be black to give the black circle on the right hand end. Then 2 must be black also for 1 and 2 to give the white on the left hand end. 2 black implies 3 white, which in turn implies 4 white, which in turn implies 5 black. But this makes 5 and 6 of opposite colours which contradict with the fact that the penultimate circle is white. Clearly a similar contradiction would have arisen if we started by letting 6 be black.

A single black circle is also impossible for it would have to arise from a black circle and a white circle and a little thought will soon show that at least one more black circle must occur.

The pattern must repeat itself at some stage for there is only a finite number of possible patterns for a row and the process goes on generating new rows ad infinitum!

21 Investigations on a 5×5 pinboard

(a)

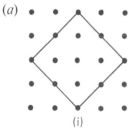
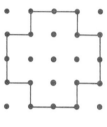
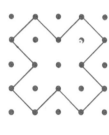

(i)   (ii)

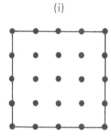
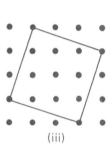
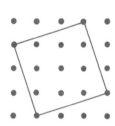

(iii)

(b) The two parallelograms intersect in a square having the required properties. Can you use a similar method to form a regular octagon surrounding 9 pins and having 16 pins outside it?

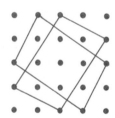

(c)

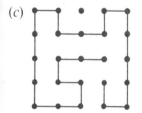
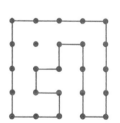
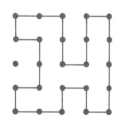

Near misses like those in the diagram initially encourage further attempts, but the fact that one pin always remains elusive leads to the realisation that it may not be possible. This can be confirmed by the following argument whose simplicity lends itself to the general case whenever there are an odd number of pins.

In this case there are 25 pins so a route which visits each once and returns to the starting pin will have 25 steps. However, for a route to return to the pin from which it started an even number of steps will be required, for every step to the right will at some stage need to be cancelled by a step to the left, every step up by a step down, and so on. These two conditions are incompatible so a solution is not possible.

22 Chess board tours

Rook's tours

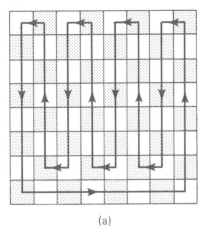
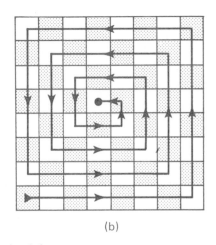

(a)   (b)

At least 15 changes of direction are required for a re-entrant tour, see (a), whilst the non re-entrant tour can be achieved with 14 changes of direction as in (b).

It is impossible for a rook to make a complete tour of the board from one corner to the opposite corner. To move from bottom left to top right the rook will undergo a displacement of 7 squares to the right and 7 squares up. That is a total of 14 squares. On the tour any further moves to the right must be balanced by equivalent moves to the left, and further moves up must be balanced by equivalent moves down. Thus, to reach the square in the top corner the rook must visit an even number of squares. But to complete the tour it must visit 63 squares. These two requirements are contradictory so the tour is impossible.

On which squares would it be possible for the rook to complete a tour having started at the bottom left hand corner?

An alternative way of seeing these activities would be as shapes which could be formed on an 8 × 8 pinboard with an elastic band which makes contact once with each pin. See Investigations on a 5 × 5 pinboard, Activity 21.

Queen's tours

Any tour, achievable by a rook is also possible with a queen so the interest here is with tours which introduce diagonal moves. A very good example of a symmetric re-entrant tour is that of the queen's magic tour. (c) is a re-entrant tour with four-fold rotational symmetry. Plenty of scope for creative mathematical thinking here.

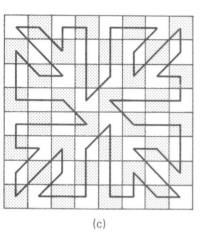

(c)

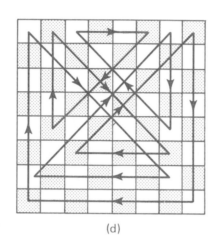

(d)

(d) is a tour that visits several squares twice but manages to tour the whole board with only thirteen changes of direction.

Bishop's tours

From a black corner square a bishop can only move in one direction so such a square cannot come in the middle of a bishop's tour. It follows that the black corners would then have to be the starting point and end point for any tour which visited all the black squares.

   Let such a tour start at the square marked 1 in (e), then as soon as the bishop has moved into square 2 only one of the squares 3 and 4 can be visited. Suppose the bishop moves to square 3, then a little thought shows that square 4 should only be reached as a last move, because there would be only one way of approaching it, that is via square

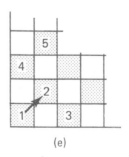

(e)

5. But we have already argued that the end point is at the far corner. Thus a complete tour is not possible.

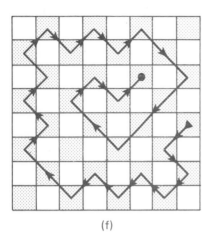

(f)

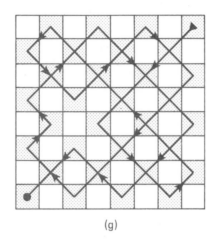

(g)

The best that can be achieved by a bishop's tour when squares cannot be revisited is 29 black squares. No matter what you do there will always be at least three black squares which are unattainable. One solution is shown in (f). The most efficient way of visiting all the black squares is shown in (g).

Knight's tours have not been discussed here as they were developed in the earlier book, *Mathematical Activities* by the author.

A very good reference for chess board puzzles and a source of many other mathematical activities is *Mathematical Recreations and Essays* by Rouse Ball.

23 Mind stretching

It is possible. The sequence of diagrams indicates how the paper model can be turned inside out and how one can imagine the hole shrinking and the tube returning to its original shape.

 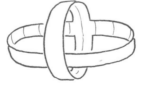 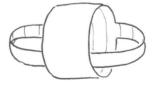 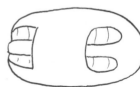

24 One step forward, march!

Many solutions are possible with a 4 × 4 board. One is shown here where A → A', B → B' etc. The 5 × 5 board however cannot be solved for the simple reason that if there are 13 black squares there will only be 12 white squares, and as a knight jumps from a black square to a white square there are just not enough vacant squares.

D'	A	C'	B
C	B'	D	A'
H'	E	G'	F
G	F'	H	E'

25 Coin magic

Moving clockwise around the square pick up the coin in the middle of each side and place on top of the next corner coin. The result is a square with a pile of two coins at each of its vertices so four coins on each side.

Easy when you know how!

26 The persistent frog

28 days.

27 Tidy that bookshelf!

The number of interchanges required depends on how muddled the books are, and a systematic way of analysing this is as follows. First put the required arrangement of the books above the given arrangement:

Required order   1   2   3   4   5   6   7   8   9
Given order   6   5   7   1   8   9   3   2   4

It then becomes clear that books 3 and 7 are in each others' positions so that a simple interchange of these, represented by (3 7), puts them right.

None of the other books are so simply displaced. On inspection we see that

       6 is in the 1 position
       1 is in the 4 position
       4 is in the 9 position
and   9 is in the 6 position

so these four books need only be interchanged among themselves. Their relative positions can be denoted by (6 1 4 9) and they can be put into their correct places by a minimum of three interchanges such as (4 9) followed by (1 4) followed by (6 1).
The remaining three books' relative positions can be similarly denoted by (5 2 8) as

       5 is in the position of 2
       2 is in the position of 8
and   8 is in the position of 5.

These can be put in their right positions by the interchange (2 8) followed by the interchange (5 2).
   Thus the encyclopaedias illustrated could be put into their correct order by the following interchanges

   (3 7) (4 9) (1 4) (6 1) (2 8) (5 2)

The solution is not unique but six interchanges is the minimum number of moves from the position given.
   Applying the same approach to the second arrangement given

Required order	1	2	3	4	5	6	7	8	9
Given order	4	5	7	6	8	1	9	2	3

we can describe the muddle as

   (4 1 6) (5 2 8) (7 3 9)

and this could be put right by a sequence of six interchanges such as

   (1 6) (4 1) (2 8) (5 2) (3 9) (7 3)

Now find the minimum number of interchanges to tidy up the order 2 3 5 9 4 1 8 6 7.

28 Square a Greek cross

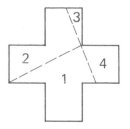 

29 The fuel delivery

Depot P I H O N M D E F G S R Q C B L K J A depot.

30 Fair shares

Fill *5* from *8*. Fill *3* from *5* leaving 2 in *5*. Empty *3* into *8*.
Pour 2 from *5* into *3*. Fill *5* from *8*.
Pour from *5* into *3* until full leaving 4 in *5*.
Empty *3* into *8* making 4 in *8* also.

31 Move a queen

The game must end in a finite number of moves as the
queens cannot retrace their steps, and each move restricts
the field of play. Not an easy game to analyse although
there is an analysis in *Winning Ways* by Berlekamp,
Conway and Guy.

Note the game can also be played so that the player who
removes the last queen is the loser.

32 Rolling cubes

Imagine the cube placed on a black square of a chessboard, then it is possible to roll it to any other black square with the letter A facing the right way up, but not to any white square.

Using the notation R, L, U and D for a roll of the cube about a bottom edge in the directions right, left, up and down, respectively, then the black square immediately to the right of the starting square can be reached by the sequence of six rolls

$$U \to U \to R \to D \to D \to R$$

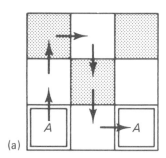

(a)

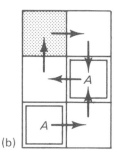

(b)

This sequence of moves can be abbreviated by the notation U^2RD^2R. This end result cannot be achieved with fewer rolls. It can also be achieved by sequences such as $LU^2R^3D^2$ or $D^2R^3U^2L$ or $LD^2R^3U^2$, all requiring eight rolls. It clearly follows, by repetition, that all the black squares in the same row can be reached, and a similar sequence of moves will enable the black squares in the same column to be reached. To make it possible to reach all black squares it is necessary to find a sequence which will move the cube to the nearest diagonal black square. This can be achieved by RULURD, as shown in (b) taking six moves, or using DRULUR, the sequence in reverse order.

Examples of minimum sequences of rolls to move the cube to the squares labelled 1 to 12 in (c) are listed below. It should be relatively straightforward to see how these can be adapted to reach any other black square.

(c)

10		11		12
	8		9	
5		6		7
	3		4	
A		1		2

1. U^2RD^2R
2. R^4
3. RULURD
4. $RDRU^3RD$
5. R^2UL^2U
6. RU^2LDR^2U
7. $R^2U^3R^2D$
8. $ULUR^3UL$
9. RURURU
10. U^4
11. $U^2R^3U^2L$
12. R^4U^4

When you have worked through the above sequences you should be in a good position to charm WARTS into STRAW.

The following solution may be the most efficient, but the author would be interested to hear from anyone who finds a better one, i.e. one involving fewer than 26 moves.

A : U²R
T : D²L
R : U
S : L²D
W : R⁴
S : UL²
T : U²L
R : D²
A : D²R
R : U

Two further problems to try are

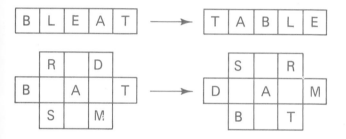

This is an excellent activity to develop spatial thinking in 3D as well as encouraging the need for systematic investigation and use of notation for recording results efficiently.

33 Make yourself a harmonograph

Watching a harmonograph trace out its patterns is a fascinating experience. Such models have become the centre of attention at many a school open day over the years, and well repay any effort required to make them. Experimenting with harmonographs gives an appreciation of damped harmonic motion which underlies many phenomena. Further, the way in which two independent oscillations working at right angles to one another can generate a variety of curves comes across very clearly. The author made his first harmonograph twenty-five years ago, having read *Mathematical Models* by Cundy and Rollett, and this book is still worth looking at. When that book was first written there was a problem in constructing a suitable pen but the advent of the ball-point has overcome that.

The paving slap harmonograph as first described is virtually fool-proof (but don't drop the slab on your toe!) and a more elaborate version of it can be made by having two paving slabs swinging close to one another with the paper on one and the pen arm pivoted on the other!

Another source of ideas on this activity is the Science Museum, South Kensington, London SW7 2DD which has produced a pamphlet entitled *How to make a twin-elliptic harmonograph*.

Peter Pan Playthings make 'Harmonograph, an amazing drawing machine for all ages' . . . but a paving slab is cheaper!

34 Make a matchbox computer

The author originally made matchbox computers with two parallel first forms at Exeter School as a class project, and they created much interest particularly when one form's computer challenged the other's, and also at an Open Day when parents were invited to play them. The activity has much deeper significance in suggesting ways in which animals (humans?) and electronic computers may learn from experience. Only one method of compensating the matchboxes has been discussed here but others may be tried out and a 'learning curve' plotted of number of games won against number of games played in each case, to aid comparison. This idea is discussed in some more detail in the SMP handbook, 'We built our own computers' which was written by a group of the author's sixth formers back in the early sixties but is now out of print.

35 More matchstick mindbenders

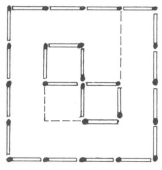
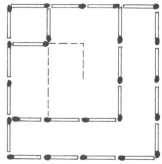

or

Spiral to squares

Church to squares

36 Tails up!

Only the first of these coin puzzles is impossible.

1   Any move from the starting point of three heads (H^3) leads to a single head and two tails (HT^2) while any move from HT^2 leads to H^3 or HT^2 again, thus only two basic arrangements are possible and the only moves from them are neatly summarised by

2   Possible in four moves. One solution is

```
H    H    H    H
H*   T    T    T
T    T*   H    H
H    H    H*   T
T    T    T    T*
```

The asterisk indicates the coin which was not turned over in the move.

You may like to investigate the possible arrangements from five coins when a move consists of turning over any four etc.

3   Possible in five moves. Label the nine coins $a, b, \ldots i$ as shown. Then one solution consists of the following moves: turn a, e, i; turn b, e, h; turn c, e, g; turn a, b, c; turn g, h, i.
Note that the order in which these moves is made makes no difference.
   Which arrangements of head and tail are possible?
   Is the puzzle still possible if diagonal moves are excluded?

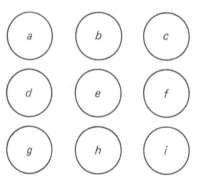

37 Dovetailed

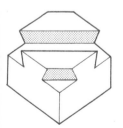 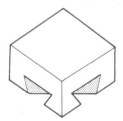

The dovetails are cut at a diagonal, not parallel to the faces of the block as the apprentices had thought.

38 Impossible rotations!

Rotate the book about an edge through 180°, then about a
line at 45° to this to obtain a 90° rotation as shown. In
general, a rotation of 180° about one axis followed by a
rotation of 180° about an axis at an angle x to it is
equivalent to a rotation through an angle $2x$ about an axis
perpendicular to the original two axes.

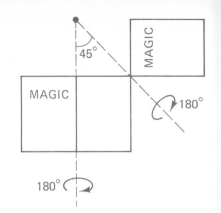

39 Problems of single line working

$a_4\ a_3\ a_2\ a_1\ A$ $B\ b_1\ b_2\ b_3\ b_4$

$a_4\ a_3\ a_2\ a_1\ A$ Bb_1b_2 $b_3\ b_4$

$B\ b_1\ b_2$ $a_4\ a_3\ a_2\ a_1\ A\ b_3\ b_4$

$B\ b_1\ b_2\ a_4\ a_3\ a_2\ a_1$ Ab_3b_4

$B\ b_1\ b_2$ b_3b_4 $a_4\ a_3\ a_2\ a_1\ A$

$B\ b_1\ b_2\ b_3\ b_4$ $a_4\ a_3\ a_2\ a_1\ A$

40 Solitaire

To describe the solutions efficiently it is helpful to have a
co-ordinate system superimposed on the solitaire board as
shown. Then A, B, C could be referred to as the holes
(2, 5), (6, 6) and (5, 2) but even more economically as
25, 66 and 52.

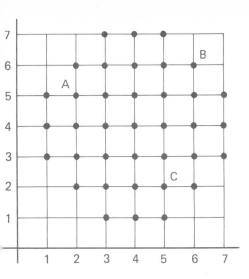

Using this notation the solutions are as follows:

The Greek cross

43 – 41   45 – 43   64 – 44 – 42   24 – 44
41 – 43 – 45   46 – 44

The diamond

55 – 75   35 – 55   42 – 44   63 – 43 – 45 –65
33 – 35 – 37 – 57 – 55 – 53 – 51 – 31 – 33 – 13 – 15 –35
75 – 55   74 – 54 – 56 – 36 – 34   24 – 44

The five crosses

64 – 62   44 – 64   74 –54   46 – 66 – 64 – 44 –46
47 – 45   24 – 26 – 46 – 44 – 24   14 – 34
42 –22 – 24 – 44 – 42   41 – 43   62 – 42 – 44

The enclosed cross

24 – 44   36 – 34   55 – 35   25 – 45   33 –35
53 – 33   23 – 43   56 – 36 – 34   73 – 53
65 – 63   53 –73   51 – 53   32 – 52   53 – 51

For further solitaire puzzles see books such as:
Mathematical Activities by Brian Bolt
Winning Ways vol. 2 by Berlekamp, Conway and Guy
Creative Puzzles of the World by P van Delft and J
Botermans
Further Mathematical Diversions by Martin Gardner.

41 All change

a	b	c	d
1	2	3	

(a)

a	b	c	d	e
1	2	3	4	

(b)

The solutions are most easily described by tracing the route of the unoccupied square.

Using the notation in diagram (a) a solution to the six coin interchange is given by

$$3\ b\ 1\ a\ 2\ c\ d$$

while the solution to the eight coin interchange (b) is

$$4\ c\ 2\ a\ 1\ b\ 3\ d\ e$$

A study of the zig-zag progress along the rows and back will soon indicate how the solution can be generalised to complete the interchange in one more move than there are coins. A smaller number of moves is impossible, for the first move must use the top right hand square which does not feature in the final position, while every other move moves each coin to its final resting place.

$$N = 2n + 1$$

Note, this activity and the next could equally well be carried out with pegs in a pegboard, pieces on a draught board, pawns on a chessboard, coloured counters on squared paper etc.

Activities like these are excellent for getting children involved in analysing patterns, and forming hypotheses and testing them.

42 Pegs progress

For a 3 × 3 board 13 moves are required.
For a 4 × 4 board 21 moves are required.
For a 5 × 5 board 29 moves are required.

$$N = 8n - 11$$

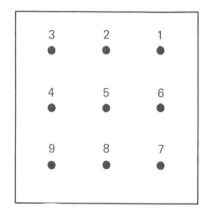

These numbers and formula may have been arrived at by much trial and error but the activity gives opportunity for some real insight.

Consider the positions in the 3 × 3 board labelled 1 to 9 as shown, then before the red peg can move, a space has to be generated next to it. This is most easily achieved by moving three pegs around the boundary so that the space moves $1 \rightarrow 2 \rightarrow 3 \rightarrow 4$, then the red peg at 9 can be moved to position 4 on the fourth move. The red peg can now be systematically moved right, up, right in a step-like path to the top corner by sequences of 3-peg moves as indicated by the following diagrams.

Right
in
three

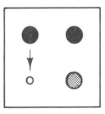
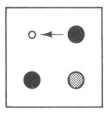
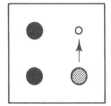

Up
in
three

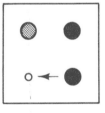
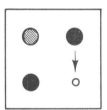
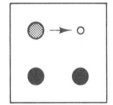

135

The path followed by the red peg, with the number of peg moves required for each step is shown below for the 3 × 3, 4 × 4, and 5 × 5 boards.

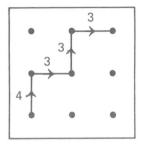
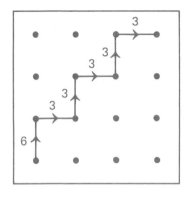
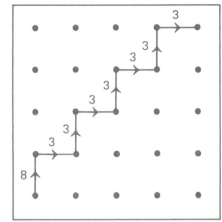

Thus for an $n \times n$ board the number of moves will be

$$N = (2n - 2) + (2n - 3) \times 3 = 8n - 11$$

Try investigating the equivalent problem on rectangular boards.

43 Pinboard triangles

Underlying this question is the very fundamental difference between rational numbers and irrational numbers. Not only is it impossible to form an equilateral triangle on any size pinboard, but it is not even possible to form one angle of 60°. Only gradients equal to rational numbers of the form $\frac{m}{n}$ are possible on a pinboard whereas $\tan 60° = \sqrt{3}$ which is irrational.

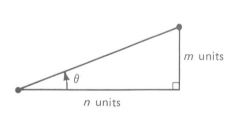
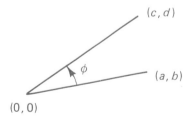

$$\tan \theta = \frac{m}{n} \neq \sqrt{3}$$

$$\tan \phi = \frac{ad - bc}{ac + bd} \neq \sqrt{3}$$

44 Rigid structures in two dimensions

The essential property of the triangle is its rigidity when seen as a physical structure, and this is of more significance to most people than its angle sum or its area. Examples of its use abound in the environment and it makes a good topic for a project.

Building a bridge across a gap using a strip of equilateral triangles is quite revealing for it shows that it is not necessary to have long girders to span a wide gap.

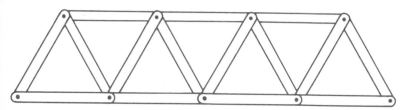

A gap of 28 cm can be spanned using 15 of the 8 cm struts as shown.

All the quadrilateral structures shown are rigid even though some movement may be possible in a model if the joints are slack. Card strips and paper fasteners are probably better for this activity than geostrips where there is often considerable play in the joints.

A hexagon can always be triangulated with 3 diagonal

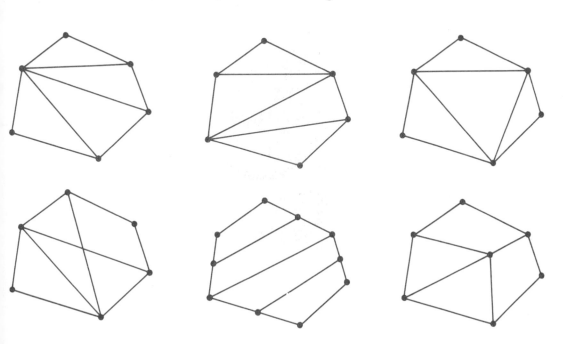

struts to make it rigid and other ways can also be found
using just 3 struts, see p.137. In general an n-sided
polygonal linkage can always be made rigid with $n-3$
additional struts and this can be investigated.

Rigidity in three dimensions is discussed in Activity 45 and
this activity can also be linked to Activity 82 on variable
base triangles. The rigidity of a triangle is the basis for
surveying and navigation so links could be made with these
topics. The essence of this activity is to see geometrical
ideas in the environment and to undertake practical
experiments to build up experiences which could be useful
for the future, apart from their immediate interest.

45 Rigid structures in three dimensions

Constructing models by threading cotton or shirring elastic
through drinking straws is a creative and instructive
experience. A needle is not essential, and may be better
avoided with young children, for the thread can easily be
pushed in at one end of a straw and sucked out of the
other . . . but don't suck too hard or you will get a
mouthful! Shirring elastic is easier to use than cotton for it
can be stretched before a knot is tied, and on shrinking
gives a good joint. Paper straws sometimes flatten and
collapse and rather than replace them they can often be
strengthened at the weak point by inserting a matchstick or
cocktail stick as a splint. Plastic straws look more
attractive and in some respects are stronger. However, the
tension on the thread can sometimes split their ends. If this
happens the end can have sticky tape wrapped around it.
   To construct a tetrahedron, or more complex model,
without having to cut the thread, it is necessary, after tying
a knot at a vertex, to take the thread back inside a straw to
the next vertex from where a straw is required. There is
satisfaction in making a model in this way, but as far as
the finished model is concerned it will make no difference.

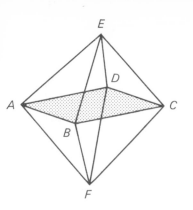
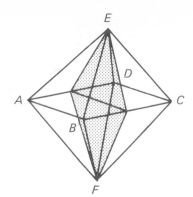
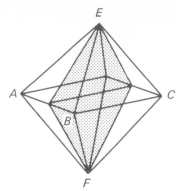

A rectangular octahedron has nine different planes of symmetry. There are three planes like *ABCD* which go through four vertices, namely

ABCD, *AECF* and *BEDF*

Then there are two planes which go through each pair of opposite vertices and bisect a pair of edges. The two through *E* and *F* are shown in the diagram, and the similar pairs through *A* and *C*, and *B* and *D*, give a total of six planes of symmetry of this kind.

When a regular tetrahedron is added to every other face of a regular octahedron, a larger tetrahedron results, whose edge is twice that of the original.

What is the volume of the octahedron compared to the volume of the tetrahedron?

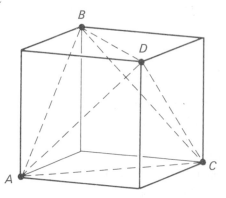

What shape is formed if a regular tetrahedron is added to all 8 faces of a regular octahedron?

A cube can be made rigid in many ways, but the neatest solution is to build a regular tetrahedron into it such as *ABCD* in the diagram. This requires six straws, each of which is a diagonal of one of the six faces of the cube. It cannot be solved with fewer straws.

We have very little experience of making structures rigid. What straws will be needed to make the following structures rigid?

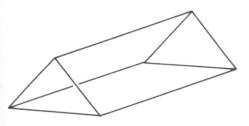

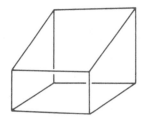

Buckminster Fuller was an eccentric genius whose unconventional approach to a wide range of problems

makes very interesting reading. Try for example *The Dymaxion World of Buckminster Fuller*, by Buckminster Fuller and Marks. A fascinating photo of one of his geodesic domes under construction is to be found in the Life Science Library, *Mathematics* volume. An interesting article showing the possibilities of straw and thread models is to be found in Volume 5, Number 4 of the journal *Mathematics in School*.

46 A lover's ultimatum!

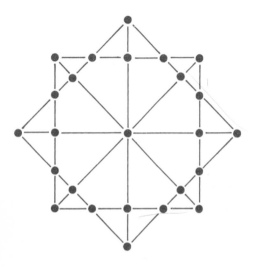

47 Only four lines!

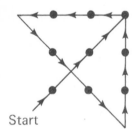

Start

Now try connecting 16 dots in a 4 × 4 array by using six straight lines without lifting your pencil from the paper.

48 Dividing the inheritance

No point exists inside the ranch from which lines can be drawn to the corners to form four triangles of equal area. It is only possible for a quadrilateral to be divided up in this way when a diagonal (*AC*) of the quadrilateral bisects its area, then the mid-point *M* of the diagonal is the required point.

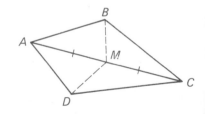

140

49 Triangulating a square

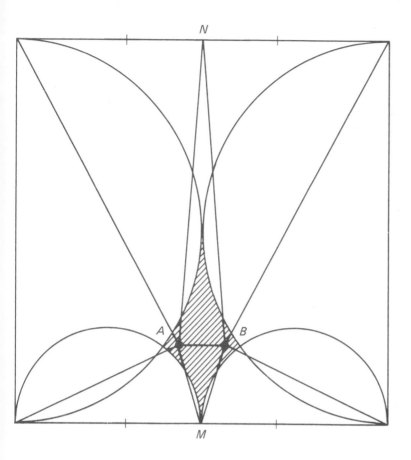

The author believed that this was not possible, but recently has been sent two neat solutions. The adjoining solution is that using the least number of triangles. It is clear from the semi-circles that points *A* and *B* can be taken anywhere inside the shaded region as long as triangles *ABM* and *ABN* are acute angled.

50 Who is 'it'?

Start at *a* and keep counting on thirteen crossing out the letter you reach. The result will be that *g* is left in at the end. Thus to leave *c* last, which is opposite *g*, start at *e*.

51 Find the cards on the table

The solution is as shown. It can be deduced in the following way.

Suppose that the face value of four adjacent cards is a, b, c, d. Then

$$b + c + d = a + b + c$$
or $b + c + d = a + b + c + 1$
or $b + c + d = a + b + c - 1$

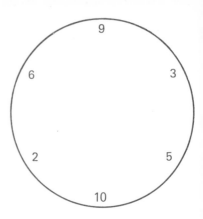

The first of these alternatives leads to $a = d$ which is not possible while the others give $d = a + 1$ or $d = a - 1$. Taking $d = a + 1$ (the other alternative leads to the same final solution) we have four adjacent cards with face values of

$a \quad b \quad c \quad a+1$

Using the same argument above to generate the face value of the next card we find it has to be $b - 1$, the next $c + 1$ and the card after that has to be a, so we are back to where we started with only the six cards

$a \quad b \quad c \quad a+1 \quad b-1 \quad c+1$

in that order around the circle.

$(a, a+1)$ $(b-1, b)$ and $(c, c+1)$ are consecutive pairs of numbers and as 2, 5, 6 and 10 are given it follows that the missing cards are 3 and 9.

52 Reafforestation!

A pegboard and plentiful supply of pegs would be an aid to solving this puzzle. The solution is very satisfying when you find it because of its symmetry.

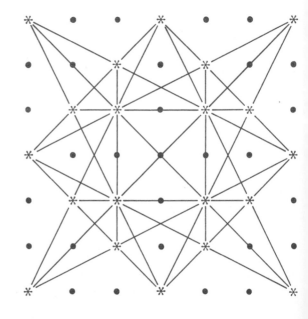

53 The rolling cube game

This game is available commercially from sources such as
David Singmaster Ltd, 66 Mount View Road, London
N4 4JR but there is no reason why you cannot make your
own. Initially it may be easier to play if, say, each cube has
5 white faces and one red face.

A very good analysis of this game, and similar games, is
to be found in the book, *Puzzle it out, cubes, groups and
puzzles*, by Ewing and Kosniowski. A fundamental
sequence of moves to come to terms with is the one which
cycles the three cubes in a corner.

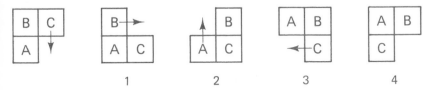

The sequence is shown here for the top left hand corner
but similar sequences apply at each corner. The effect of
this sequence brings a different set of faces to the top and
it is combinations of sequences of this kind which lead to
the puzzle's solution.

54 Two at a time

Put 7 on 10, 5 on 2, 3 on 8, 1 on 4, 9 on 6.

As the end point has to be piles of two coins, only lines
containing an even number of coins need be considered.
Two coins do not lend themselves to a solution, but any
other even number of coins can be solved as follows.

4 coins

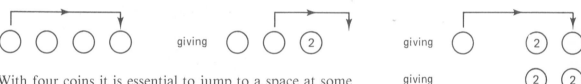

With four coins it is essential to jump to a space at some
stage so that three moves will be the minimum.

6 coins

Again, experimenting will show that a solution cannot be achieved without jumping into a space. When this is realised, one move can be made which reduces the solution to that of four coins in a row giving a total of four moves.

8 coins

With eight coins it is possible to pair off all the coins in four moves as shown, without the waste of moving into a space in the sequence.

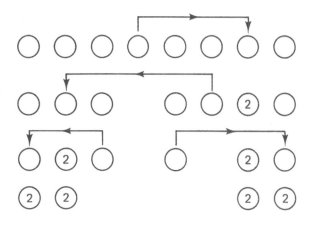

$2n$ coins ($n \geqslant 4$)

For $2n$ coins when $n \geqslant 4$ it is always possible to achieve n piles of 2 coins in n moves. This is easily seen by using an inductive argument, which reduces the problem in well defined steps to one already solved. Consider the case of 14 coins to illustrate the argument.

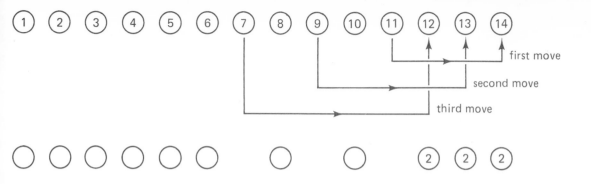

First move 11 onto 14, then 9 onto 13, followed by 7 onto 12 to form three piles of two coins at the end and leaving a line of eight single coins which can be solved as above. This is a nice introduction to an inductive argument which could easily be turned into a formal mathematical proof.

55 The prisoner's perambulations

This is an excellent activity to promote 3D thinking.

Some sort of simplified diagram of the situation or a model, made from straws and pipe cleaners, say, to represent the corridors and staircases will certainly help, as will a notation to record the routes.

When no staircase is climbed twelve routes are possible.

These routes are all indicated below where the numbers refer to the diagram.

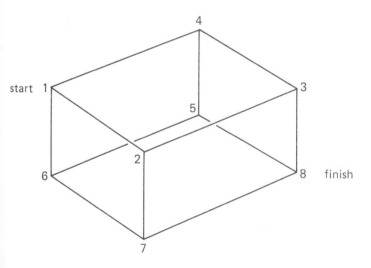

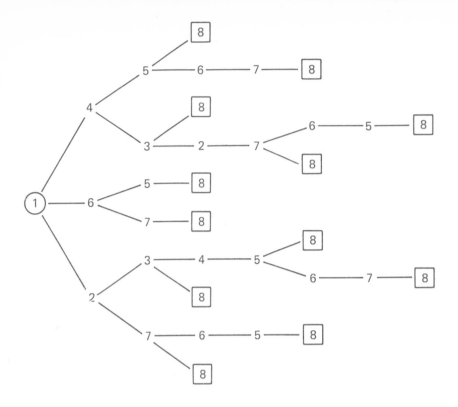

There are six further routes possible when the staircases can be climbed, namely

1 – 4 – 5 – 6 – 7 – 2 – 3 – 8
1 – 2 – 7 – 6 – 5 – 4 – 3 – 8
1 – 6 – 7 – 2 – 3 – 8
1 – 6 – 5 – 4 – 3 – 8
1 – 6 – 7 – 2 – 3 – 4 – 5 – 8
1 – 6 – 5 – 4 – 3 – 2 – 7 – 8

Note that the solutions go in pairs about the plane 1386.

This activity can be extended in a variety of ways, for example:
How many routes are possible if the princess can revisit the tower rooms, but not travel along any corridor or staircase twice? How many routes are possible for the princess to the room immediately beneath her own?
How many routes would be possible between two given points if the princess had access to three floors?

Try investigating similar problems with castles having a different number of towers and see if you can discover any general pattern which might be expressed as a formula.

56 Crossed lines

(*a*) 6   (*b*) 30

When the number of power stations and towns is small then the answers can be found by careful drawing. However the formula

$$n = \frac{1}{4} p(p - 1) \, t(t - 1)$$

shows that the number of crossed lines rises very rapidly.

One approach to seeing where the formula comes from is as follows:

$$p = 2 \qquad t = 10$$

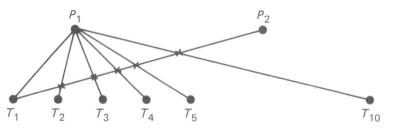

Imagine all the lines drawn from P_1 to $T_1, T_2, \ldots, T_{10}$ then the line $P_2 T_1$ crosses nine lines, the line $P_2 T_2$ crosses eight lines and so on until $P_2 T_9$ crosses just one line. Thus when there are two power stations and ten towns the number of crossed lines is given by

$$9 + 8 + 7 + 6 + 5 + 4 + 3 + 2 + 1.$$

This leads to the formula

$$n = \frac{1}{2} t(t - 1) \text{ whenever } p = 2.$$

If a third power station P_3 is introduced then the lines from it to t towns will cross the lines from P_1 at $\frac{1}{2} t(t - 1)$ places and the lines from P_2 also at $\frac{1}{2} t(t - 1)$ places. A fourth power station P_4 when joined to the t towns will cross the lines from P_1, from P_2 and from P_3 each in $\frac{1}{2} t(t - 1)$ places, and so on leading to

$$n = \frac{1}{2} t(t - 1) [1 + 2 + 3 + \ldots (p - 1)] \text{ for}$$

p power stations

$$= \frac{1}{2} t(t - 1) \times \frac{1}{2} p(p - 1).$$

147

57 Bridging the river

Try experimenting with a pile of dominoes to represent the
sleepers. With 3 sleepers the best which can be achieved is
$3\frac{2}{3}$ metres. The smallest number of sleepers which will
enable the structure to overlap the opposite bank, 5 metres
away, is 7.

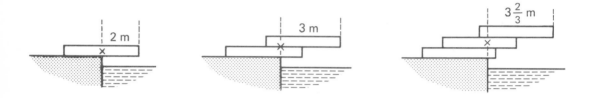

To understand how the solution is reached consider the
sequence of diagrams. With one sleeper it can clearly be
pushed out across the river for a distance of 2 metres, to
the point at which its centre of mass is immediately over
the edge of the bank. With two sleepers, the top sleeper
can similarly overlap the bottom sleeper by 2 metres before
it tips, and the bottom sleeper remains stable as long as the
centre of mass of both sleepers taken together (shown with
a cross in the diagram) is at the river's edge. A little
thought will show that this gives an extra 1 metre to the
overhang giving a total overhang of 3 metres.

When a third sleeper is introduced, the top two sleepers
can overhang the bottom one by 3 metres, and the bottom
sleeper is arranged so that the combined centre of mass of
the three sleepers is at the river's edge. In this case the
bottom sleeper protrudes over the river $\frac{2}{3}$ metre.

Each successive sleeper extends the bridge but by smaller
and smaller amounts leading to the following formula for
the maximum overhang (d) when n sleepers are used

$$d = 2 \left(1 + \tfrac{1}{2} + \tfrac{1}{3} + \tfrac{1}{4} + \tfrac{1}{5} + \ldots + \tfrac{1}{n}\right) \text{ metres}$$

When $n = 6$
$$d = 2 \left(1 + \tfrac{1}{2} + \tfrac{1}{3} + \tfrac{1}{4} + \tfrac{1}{5} + \ldots + \tfrac{1}{6}\right) = 4.9 \text{ metres}$$

Which just falls short of the far bank, but when $n = 7$

$$d = 4.9 + \frac{2}{7} \simeq 5.19 \text{ metres}$$

To the mathematician the above formula is fascinating for it indicates that given a sufficient number of sleepers it is theoretically possible to build a structure on one bank which will overlap the far bank no matter how wide the river may be.

58 Crossing the desert

To exceed 600 miles, a minimum of eleven journeys would be required. Mathematically the problem is equivalent to the previous river bridging one, and a careful analysis leads to a very similar formula:

$$d = 200 \left(1 + \frac{1}{2} + \frac{1}{3} + \frac{1}{4} + \frac{1}{5} + \ldots + \frac{1}{n}\right) \text{ miles}$$

where d is the maximum penetration possible with n lorry journeys.

To see how the formula comes about, first consider the best solution possible with two lorry journeys.

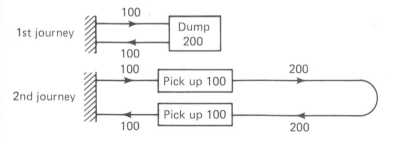

The loaded lorry first travels 100 miles into the desert, dumps 200 miles' worth of provisions and just makes it back to base. It then reloads and travels 100 miles to the dump where it can take on 100 miles' worth of provision, to replenish what is used up getting there, and is then able to do a further 200 miles into the desert and back arriving at the dump having used all its resources. However at the dump is just the 100 miles' worth of provisions needed to get the lorry back to base. Thus the lorry has been able to penetrate 300 miles into the desert.

Now consider the situation with n lorry journeys and $n - 1$ dumps $D_1, D_2, \ldots, D_{n-1}$ distances $d_1, d_2, \ldots, d_n$, as shown in the diagram.

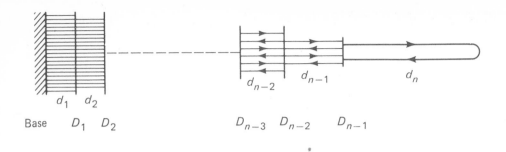

The total number of journeys between any neighbouring pair of dumps decreases by two, as the dumps advance into the desert, so that the total distance travelled by the lorry in n journeys, assuming all the fuel etc. has been used up when it finally returns to base, is

$$400n = 2d_n + 4d_{n-1} + 6d_{n-2} + \ldots 2(n-1)d_2 + 2nd_1$$

But we also know that

$$400(n-1) = 2d_n + 4d_{n-1} + 6d_{n-2} + \ldots + 2(n-1)d_2$$

as this corresponds to the situation with $n-1$ lorry journeys. Hence

$$400n - 400(n-1) = 2nd_1 \text{ which gives } d_1 = \frac{200}{n}$$

The following table gives the distance to the first dump from the base, and the maximum distance travelled into the desert for different numbers of journeys.

No of journeys	1	2	3	4	5	6	7	8
Dist. to 1st dump		100	66.7	50	40	33.3	28.6	25
Max. dist. into desert	200	300	367	417	457	490	519	544

Similar problems to this and to activity 57 are discussed in *Puzzle-math* by Gamow and Stern and *Ingenious Mathematical Problems* by Graham.

59 Can you help the motorway designer?

Interestingly the shortest route is as shown, where the motorway has two 3-way junctions, and the roads all meet at 120°. Simple trigonometry shows that the length of this motorway would be 54.6 miles. This solution can be strikingly shown using a soap film stretched between four pins at the vertices of a square between two perspex plates. The solutions of other similar shortest route problems can be demonstrated in this way and often have very surprising solutions. An analysis of these problems, often called Steiner problems after the German mathematician who drew attention to them, is to be found in the book *What is Mathematics?* by Courant and Robbins.

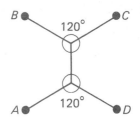

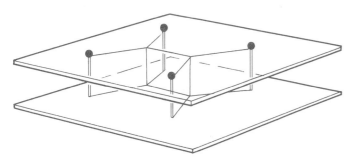

60 Who nobbled the racehorse?

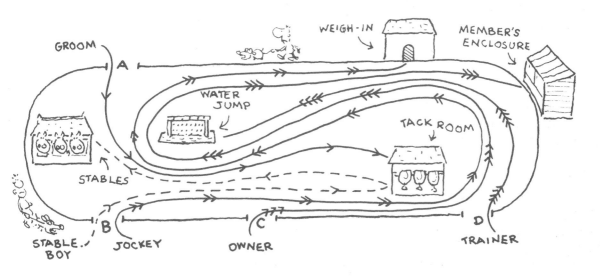

Putting all the evidence available on the diagram of the racecourse leads to the groom as being the guilty party. The jockey's route excludes the owner and the trainer, while the fact that the stable lad and the groom met at the tack room excludes the jockey.

61 Court card capers

One solution is

Ah	Kc	Qd	Js
Qs	Jd	Ac	Kh
Jc	Qh	Ks	Ad
Kd	As	Jh	Qc

which satisfies all the requirements.

This puzzle is of very long standing for it has existed in a published form from early in the eighteenth century. Euler, the celebrated mathematician, proposed a similar puzzle concerning 36 army officers, six from each of six regiments. But this was later shown to be insoluble. However, should you wish to try another problem of this type which has a solution consider the following.

In a saloon car race there were five teams A, B, C, D and E each with five cars labelled 1, 2, 3, 4 and 5. The starting grid had five rows and the cars were five abreast in a 5 × 5 array. To make the start as fair to each team as possible it was arranged that in any row, or column, or diagonal of the starting grid there would be only one car from each team, and only one car with each number. Find a suitable starting position for the cars.

Problems of this type are based on Eulerian Squares which are discussed briefly in *Mathematical Recreations and Essays* by Rouse Ball.

62 Heads and tails

Initially			H	T	H	T	H	T	H	T
First move	T	H	H	T	H	T	H			T
Second move	T	H	H	T			H	H	T	T
Third move	T			T	H	H	H	H	T	T
Fourth move	T	T	T	T	H	H	H	H		

63 The chapel hymnboard

Only 51 cards are necessary.

Because of the possibility of someone choosing the five hymns

966   699   696   669   666

The 6 (9) digit will have to occur in fifteen different cards.

Because of the possibility of someone choosing five hymns such as

888   881   882   883   884

all the digits 8, 7, 5, 4, 3, 2, 1 will have to occur on eleven different cards.

The largest number of occurrences of 0 will be with a selection of hymns such as

100   200   300   400   500

so that 0 will have to occur on ten different cards.

This gives a total of 102 numbers, and by careful pairing of these it will be possible to put them onto 51 cards and satisfy all requirements.

Such a solution would be as follows.

Two cards each of (6, 1) (6, 2) (6, 3) (6, 4) (6, 5) (6, 7) (6, 8)
One card   (6, 0)
Four cards   (0, 8)
Five cards   (8, 7)
Four cards   (7, 5)
Five cards   (5, 4)
Four cards   (4, 3)
Five cards   (3, 2)
Four cards   (2, 1)
Five cards   (1, 0)

64 Find the radius of the circle

Nothing to it unless you are misled by the surplus information. As $ABCO$ is a rectangle $OB = AC = 7$ cm so the radius of the circle is 7 cm.

What does the length AD determine? Can it have any positive value?

65 As easy as ABC

Intelligent use of trial and error starting with possible values for A and deducing possible values for B soon leads to the solution $A = 1$, $B = 4$, $C = 8$. This is the only solution unless you count $A = B = C = 0$.

66 Fill the corners

The simplest solution is to fill the circle in a corner with the number in the middle of the opposite side. Each side will then contain 10, 17 and 45 so have a total of 72. All other solutions are obtained by increasing these numbers by the same increment d, so the general solution will be of the form

top corner, $17 + d$: left hand corner, $45 + d$:
right hand corner, $10 + d$

giving a total along each side of $72 + 2d$. d can of course be positive or negative.

67 The end of the world!

Surprising as it may seem the first day of a century can never occur on a Sunday, a Tuesday or a Thursday. In 1582 to improve the accuracy of the calendar, Pope Gregory XIII decreed that instead of every fourth year being a leap year an exception would be made for centurial years not divisible by 400. Thus 2000 is a leap year but the years 2100, 2200 and 2300 would not be even though they are divisible by 4.

To see what effect this has on century days consider the number of days from January 1st on one century day to January 1st in the next century. There are 100 years which would normally contain 25 leap years and hence 36525 days which is equivalent to 5217 weeks and 6 days. Thus from one century day to the next, without Pope Gregory's adjustment, the weekday would move on by 6. However this only happens when a century day follows on from a century divisible by 400. When this is not the case there will only be 24 leap years in the intervening century so the day will only move on by 5. A little calculation will soon show that the century day in the year 2000 is a Saturday. Then

Year	2000		2100		2200		2300		2400		2500
Century day	Sat		Fri		Wed		Mon		Sat		Fri
		+6		+5		+5		+5		+6	

This cycle of events continues so that the century day never falls on a Sunday, Tuesday or Thursday.

The end is not in sight!

68 How many will you take?

This is an interesting game because it is subject to analysis and a player having analysed the game should easily outplay a player who has not.

A player, to win, must leave his opponent eventually with 1 counter. To do this, at his penultimate move, he must leave 5 counters, for if he leaves 2, 3 or 4 counters his opponent could always take away 1, 2 or 3 counters to leave one. On the other hand, if he left 6, 7 or 8 counters his opponent could leave him with 5 and a losing position.

A similar line of reasoning shows that it is 'safe' to leave totals of 9, 13, 17, 21, . . ., $4n + 1$, for no matter what his opponent's play is from one of these totals he can always play to leave the next smaller pile in the sequence . . . until his opponent is faced with removing the last counter.

The player knowing this underlying strategy will normally beat his opponent for if he finds himself starting with an 'unsafe' total such as 19 counters he can remove 2 counters to leave a 'safe' total and be sure of winning if from then on he arranges his play to complement his opponent's so that they jointly remove 4 counters at each stage.

The only time he may be in trouble is if the initial number of counters is 'safe', then his optimum strategy would be to remove only one counter in the hope that his opponent will sooner or later unwittingly leave an 'unsafe' total. Alternatively he could let his opponent start first.

How would the strategy need to be modified if a player could remove 1, 2, 3 or 4 counters at each turn?

The game could perhaps be made more interesting by letting one player decide who plays first and the other decide how many counters will be removed.

69 Envelopes of curves

To save time in this investigation it helps to use a
photocopier or other means to make several copies of a
circle marked off with 36 points. This investigation also
nicely illustrates the way in which a number pattern turns
itself into a geometric pattern. For anyone enjoying curve
stitching this activity should suggest several new ideas.

Other envelopes are to be found in Activity 70 on
forming ellipses, and Activity 71 on parabolas.

70 Four more ways to form an ellipse

In *Mathematical Activities* several methods of drawing
ellipses were discussed but the four methods here are all
quite different from those and rely on entirely different
techniques. Much is gained by just reproducing the
drawings given, but for a good A-level candidate it is an
interesting exercise to justify, in each case, why the
resulting figure is an ellipse or an envelope of one.

71 Parabolas

Curve-stitching interesting patterns based on the second
method for producing an envelope of a parabola is well
known so not pursued here. However, drawing in the
chords for $n \to 11 - n$ where n takes only the values 1, 2,
. . ., 10 can mislead anyone into thinking that the parabola
tends to the original lines when in fact its direction
approaches that of the axis of symmetry as you move
further from the vertex. To see this it is necessary to take
negative as well as positive values for n as shown in the
figure, where the original lines have been drawn at right
angles.

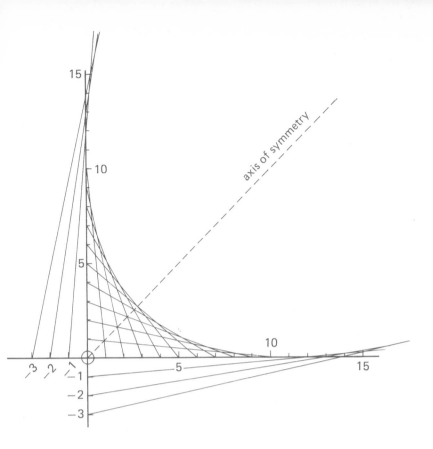

As n takes larger and larger negative values the slopes of the lines forming the envelope, which are $\frac{n}{n-11}$ and $\frac{n-11}{n}$, both approach 1. For example when $n = -1000$ the gradients of the two lines will be $\frac{1000}{1011}$ and $\frac{1011}{1000}$ which would hardly be discernable from the slope of the axis of symmetry.

A practical experiment can show how a parabolic bowl concentrates the rays of heat emitted by the sun. Make a large parabolic reflector by sticking aluminium foil into a parabolic framework made from pieces of hardboard or thick card. Suspend a test tube of water at its focus, and note how it heats up.

72 The snowflake curves

The snowflake curves are due to von Koch who invented them to show that a curve could have infinite length but contain a finite area.

With both the snowflake and anti-snowflake curves the change from one curve in the sequence to the next multiplies its perimeter by a factor of $\frac{4}{3}$ as the middle third of each edge is replaced by two new edges each equal in length to $\frac{1}{3}$ of the original.

Thus the lengths of corresponding snowflake and anti-snowflake curves are equal, and the length of the tenth will be $(\frac{4}{3})^{10}L$, while the nth will be $(\frac{4}{3})^{n}L$.

The areas of the first two snowflake curves are

$\frac{4}{3}A$ and $\frac{40}{27}A$

and in general

$$A_n = A_{n-1} + \left(\frac{4}{3}\right)^{n-1} \frac{A}{3^n}$$

where A_n is the area inside the nth snowflake curve.

Similarly the areas of the first two anti-snowflake curves are

$\frac{2}{3}A$ and $\frac{14}{27}A$

and the general formula is

$$A_n = A_{n-1} - \left(\frac{4}{3}\right)^{n-1} \frac{A}{3^n}$$

For further reading on these and other sequences of curves see *Riddles in Mathematics* by Northrop, and *Mathematical Models* by Cundy and Rollett.

The idea of processes which go on and on and the concept of a limit, which is intrinsic in this activity, is fundamental to the study of mathematics, and it is ideas like these which often capture the imagination of the embryo mathematician.

73 The staircase paradox

The staircase and snake curves only *appear* to approximate to straight lines. The staircase is always of length 2 and the snake of length $\frac{1}{2}\pi$.

74 Historical estimates for π

The following gives the estimates for π in increasing order of accuracy.

3			Old Testament Jews
$\frac{49}{16}$	=	3.0625	Baudhayana
$\sqrt{10}$	=	3.1622777	Brahmagupta
$\frac{256}{81}$	=	3.1604938	Rhind papyrus
$\frac{3}{4}(\sqrt{3} + \sqrt{6})$	=	3.1361554	Cusa
$\frac{1440}{458\frac{1}{2}}$	=	3.140676	Leonardo
$3\frac{10}{71}$	=	3.140845	Archimedes
$3\frac{1}{7}$	=	3.1428571	Archimedes
$3 + \frac{8}{60} + \frac{30}{3600}$	=	3.141667	Ptolemy
$\frac{754}{240}$	=	3.141667	Bhaskafa
$\frac{62832}{200000}$	=	3.1416	Arya-Bhata
$\frac{3927}{1250}$	=	3.1416	Bhaskafa

But by far the best historical estimate was that by the Chinese astronomer Tsu Ch'ung-Chih of $\frac{355}{113} = 3.1415929$.

75 What was the sum?

$13 \div 29 = 0.4482759$ on a calculator. These questions are easy to set!

76 Prelude to a marathon

Several solutions, but all involve a carry. One solution is

$$
\begin{array}{r}
154 \\
+ \ 782 \\
\hline
936
\end{array}
$$

and others can be obtained from it by interchanging suitable pairs of numbers such as

$$
\begin{array}{r}
152 \\
+ \ 784 \\
\hline
936
\end{array}
\qquad
\begin{array}{r}
215 \\
+ \ 478 \\
\hline
693
\end{array}
\qquad
\begin{array}{r}
278 \\
+ \ 415 \\
\hline
693
\end{array}
$$

How many possible solutions are there?

77 Dr Numerati's telephone number

$$37 \times 41 \times 43 = 65\,231$$

so Dr Numerati lived in number 41 and 65231 was her telephone number.

78 A magic diamond

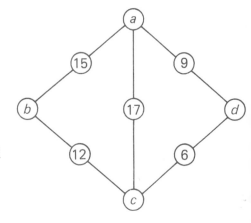

The numbers will be of the form

$$
\begin{aligned}
a &= x \\
b &= 5 + x \\
c &= 3 + x \\
d &= 11 + x
\end{aligned}
$$

where x is any number and the total along each line will then be $20 + 2x$.

   For example, if $x = 1$ then $a = 1$, $b = 6$, $c = 4$, $d = 12$ and each line total will be 22.

79 Palindromic dates

In a year such as 1982 every month apart from October or December will have a palindromic date on the 28th of the month, for example 28.6.82. In addition 1982 contains the palindromic date 2.8.82, so in all it contains eleven palindromic dates.

   We are now in for a lean time however as the only palindromic date in 1983 is 3.8.83 with similar August dates up to 9.8.89.

The closest palindromic dates will be obtained by finding the right juxtaposition of dates with a 2-digit day and a single digit day in the same or adjacent months.

Two good solutions

1.2.21 followed by 12.2.21

and 22.1.22 followed by 2.2.22

with gaps of eleven days, but the best solution would seem to be

29.8.92 followed by 2.9.92

with a gap of only four days.

80 The sponsored marathon

Each sponsor had agreed to pay

$$(1 + 2 + 4 + 8 + 16 + \ldots + 2^{25}) \text{ pence.}$$

This is £671 109 or the equivalent of £25 811 for every mile run. Let us hope that every person who sponsored this particular runner was a millionaire!

81 A calculator crossword

This and similar crosswords rarely fail to motivate children or adults. They are fun to do, but the more useful activity is to get children in groups designing their own crosswords. See *Mathematical Activities* by Brian Bolt, Activities 120, 122; also Activity 127 in this book.

■	**1** O	**2** S	**3** L	**4** O	■
5 B	■	**6** H	O	B	■
7 I	**8** S	L	E	■	E
9 B	E	■	L	■	S
10 L	E	**11** S	L	**12** I	E
E	■	I	■	L	■
■	**13** B	O	**14** I	L	**15** S
■	**16** E	S	S	O	

83 Multiplying by three

The understanding of any mechanism depends on an appreciation of how shapes interact with each other as they move. So much traditional geometry was concerned with static figures, whereas the appreciation of spatial concepts requires the ability to move shapes around in one's imagination. This ability is best acquired by making models which can be manipulated and which allow experiments to be carried out. All mechanisms have an input and an output, and in many mechanisms where the input and output are the same kind of motion (e.g. both rotary) it is meaningful to compare the two by a scale factor. Thus this activity is essentially practical – most of the apparatus required should be readily available in any secondary school but much can be done using such things as cotton reels for pulleys or winding drums.

As the linkage of rhombuses moves along a straight line, the path of P will be part of a circle with centre at O and radius OP while the paths of Q and R will be on ellipses which can be seen as obtained by stretching the circle three times and five times.

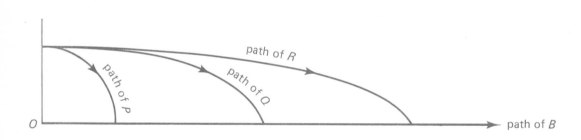

Many linkages are possible which scale up a linear movement by a factor of three. Some of these are shown below and were originally found by the author while experimenting with a box of geostrips. The first solution is based on the pantograph while the others can be seen as derived from it.

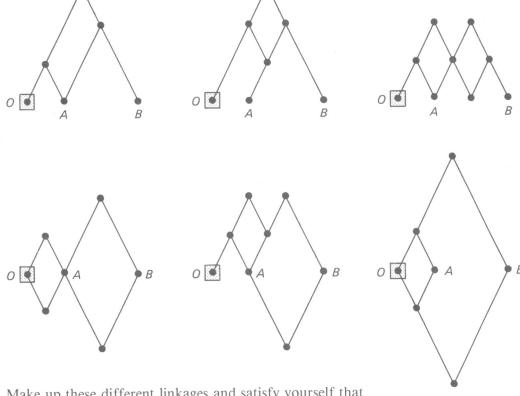

Make up these different linkages and satisfy yourself that they all have a multiplying factor of three.

The conjurer's 'string factory' has many possible solutions but the essential ingredient is that it has two winding drums. One drum has the ingoing string wrapped around it, while the other holds the outgoing string. For anyone with a Meccano set this should be an easy project, but a little ingenuity with different size cotton reels, and a pencil as axle, works quite well inside a shoe box.

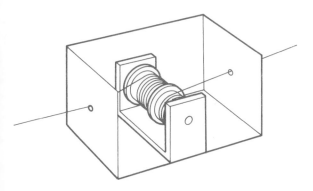

For further ideas on mechanisms see *Machines, Mechanisms and Mathematics*, published for the Schools Council Mathematics for the Majority Project by Chatto and Windus.

84 The hydrocarbons

Although this activity is set in a chemical context the underlying ideas are spatial and closely linked with constructing networks involving only 4-nodes and 1-nodes. The detailed study of organic chemistry from which these ideas arise is often left to the sixth form, yet the structure of the hydrocarbon molecules is particularly systematic, and the pattern of the alkane molecules, for example, is easy to appreciate at a much earlier stage. If a molecular building set can be borrowed from the chemistry department then the 3D structure of the molecules can be investigated, but as an exercise in topology all that is required is paper, pencil and some spatial thinking.

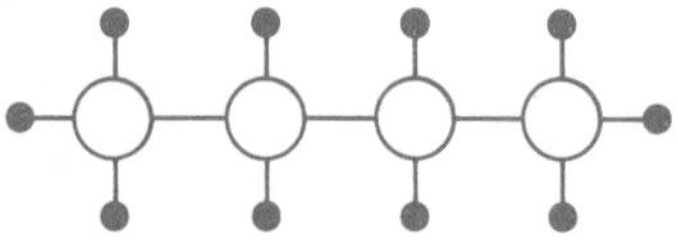

Butane C_4H_{10}

Octane C_8H_{18}

Higher alkanes $C_{17}H_{36}$, $C_{18}H_{38}$, $C_{19}H_{40}$, $C_{20}H_{42}$.

In general the alkane molecules are C_nH_{2n+2}.

The possible structures for C_6H_{14}, in addition to the one given, are shown below.

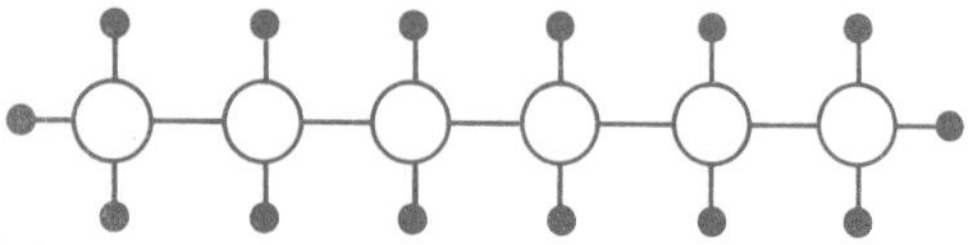

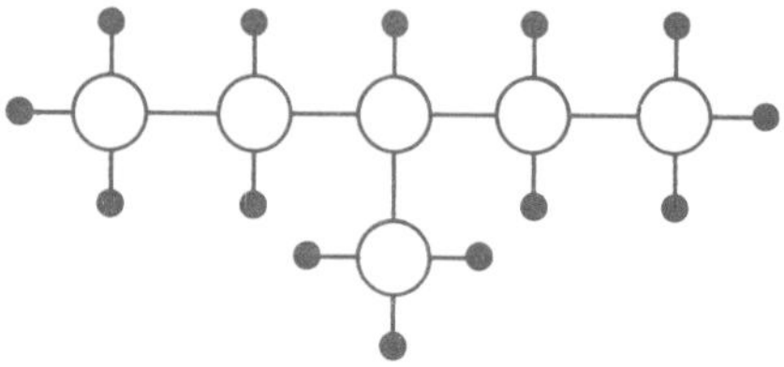

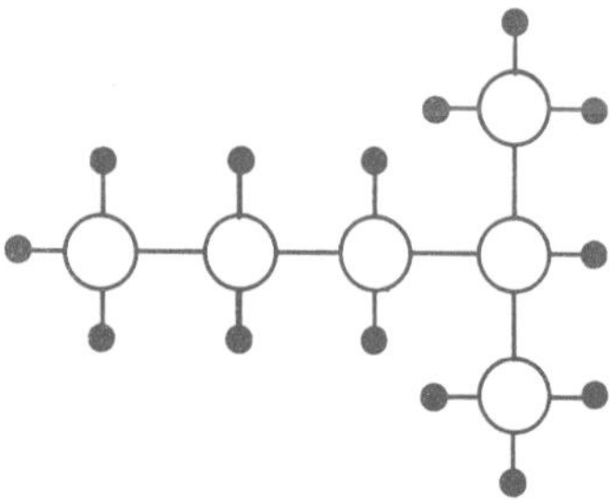

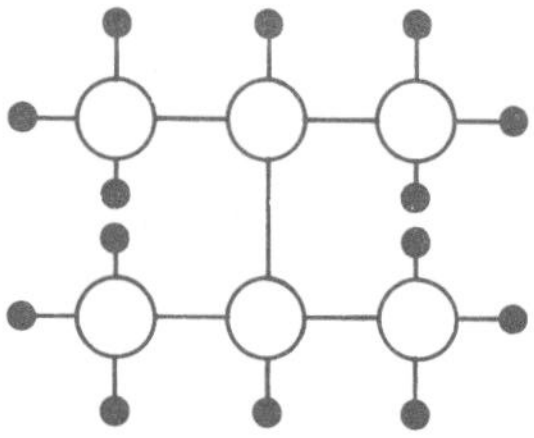

With molecules of this kind the number of hydrogen atoms is always two more than twice the number of carbon atoms, whether the carbon chains are branched or not. Why? For this reason it is only necessary to concentrate on

the different arrangements for seven carbon atoms when
seeking the possible structures for C_7H_{16}. See the diagram
for the nine solutions.

When rings of carbon atoms, together with double and
triple bonds, are considered the number of possible
molecules with just four carbon atoms and varying
numbers of hydrogen atoms is surprisingly large. The
diagrams on page 166 show 31 solutions. Only the links
between the carbon atoms are shown. Hydrogen atoms
must be added to make up the four arms of each carbon
atom which are not already linked to another carbon atom.

Note that although all these molecules seem theoretically
possible from the point of view considered, there may be
physical reasons why they do not exist in practice.

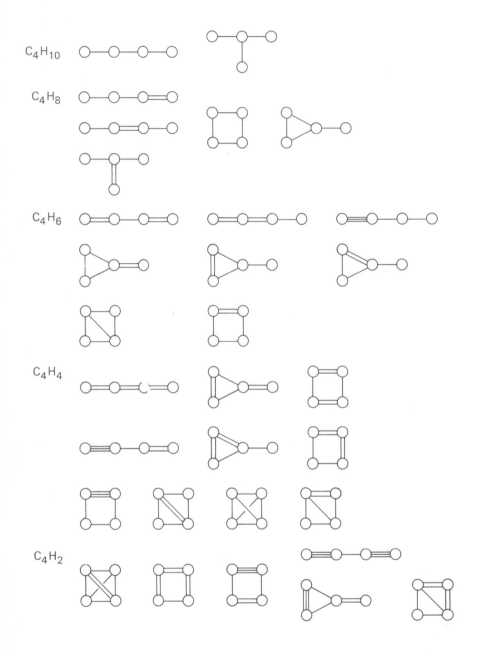

C_4H_{10}

C_4H_8

C_4H_6

C_4H_4

C_4H_2

85 Designing a new dartboard

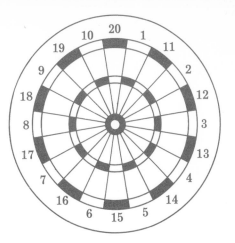

The solution shown here maximises the sum of the differences between adjacent numbers. Here there are

        10 gaps of 10
         9 gaps of 9
  and 1 gap of 19

giving a total of 200.

In general, if n is an even number, the numbers 1, 2, 3, ... n can be placed around a circle so that the sum of the gaps is $\frac{1}{2} n^2$.

What arrangement of the numbers would minimise the sum of the differences?

A good discussion of this activity is to be found in the October 1976 issue of the *Mathematical Gazette*.

86 The car importer

This puzzle depends on the fact that 1 111 111 is the product of just two prime factors: 4649 and 239. Thus there were 239 new cars each costing £4649. Theoretically 4649 cars at £239 is a possible but unrealistic answer.

87 Look before you leap!

It is easy to get caught by these and similar questions if you haven't met them before.

1 They both weigh a hundredweight.
2 A hole contains no earth.
3 The ship rises with the tide so the mayoress was faced with 12 rungs to climb.
4 40p not 80p.
5 One rabbit, the dead one.

88 Find the digits

```
  7641
− 1467
  ────
  6174
```

Many sets of four letters can be permuted to form a variety of words as, for example:

    EVIL   LIVE   VILE   VEIL   LEVI,

but not many can be found where three of the words fit the above number pattern exactly. One further example is

```
  ABLE
− ELBA
  ────
  BEAL
```

89 The effect of inflation

The formula connecting the rate of inflation $r\%$, the initial price P and the final price P_n after n years of inflation is

$$P_n = (1 + \tfrac{r}{100})^n P$$

Thus for the house price

$$34\,000 = (1 + \tfrac{r}{100})^{20} \times 3500$$

Using a calculator gives $1 + \tfrac{r}{100} = 1.120\,393\,4$
from which the rate of inflation is about 12%.

Similarly, for the cost of petrol

$$184 = (1 + \tfrac{r}{100})^{18} \times 33$$

which gives $1 + \tfrac{r}{100} = 1.100\,173\,9$
from which the rate of inflation is about 10%.

If these rates of inflation should continue then in the year 2000 the house will cost £294 794 and a gallon of petrol will be 933p.

90 Octogenarian occupations

$8^3 − 7^3 = 512 − 343 = 169 = 13^2$
The retired teacher was 87 and his great granddaughter was 13.

91 Prime factors

$$11 = 11$$
$$111 = 3 \times 37$$
$$1\,111 = 11 \times 101$$
$$11\,111 = 41 \times 271$$
$$111\,111 = 3 \times 7 \times 11 \times 13 \times 37$$
$$1\,111\,111 = 239 \times 4649$$
$$11\,111\,111 = 11 \times 73 \times 101 \times 137$$
$$111\,111\,111 = 3^2 \times 37 \times 333667$$

92 Remove a rectangle

This game can easily be played on spotty paper or squared paper or, perhaps even better, on a geo-board using elastic bands.

The person who starts should win, but the strategy is not at all obvious unless the starting array is a square. In this case the starting player should choose the diagonal point nearest to the top right-hand corner and then mirror every move his opponent makes. A win is assured as a study of the diagram below will indicate. Again A moves first.

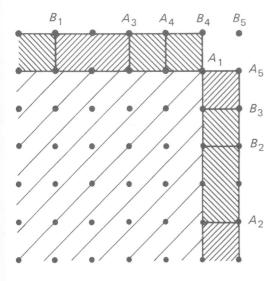

93 Subtraction to addition

The reason the method works becomes clear from the following:
$$573 - 489 = 573 + (1000 - 1000) - 489$$
$$= 573 + (999 + 1 - 1000) - 489$$
$$= 573 + (999 - 489) + 1 - 1000$$

The method is analogous to that used by computers to carry out subtraction, but there the numbers are stored in binary form. Thus instead of subtracting from a string of '9's, a string of '1's is used.

This operation is remarkably easy to perform as its effect is to change a '1' to a '0', and a '0' to a '1'. For example, $1111 - 1011 = 0100$.

Thus to find the result of $1100 - 1011$

1100	first	1111	next	1100
-1011	$\rightarrow$	-1011	$\rightarrow$	$+0100$
		$\overline{0100}$		$\overline{10000}$

and finally $\cancel{1}0\,000 + 1 = 1$

Investigate this method of subtraction in other number bases.

94 A Russian two-step

The method works because the halving process and selection of the odd numbers is essentially the process of converting the first number to a binary form. With the example discussed the remainders which are left at each stage are 1, 1, 1, 0, 0, 1 in that order from the top. Now

$$39 = 2^5 + 0 \times 2^4 + 0 \times 2^3 + 1 \times 2^2 + 1 \times 2^1 + 1$$
$$= 100111 \text{ in binary notation.}$$

Thus 39_2 is formed by taking the remainders in reverse order.

$$39 \times 79 = (2^5 \times 79) + (2^2 \times 79) + (2 \times 79) + (1 \times 79)$$
$$= 2528 + 316 + 158 + 79$$
$$= \text{the sum of the numbers produced in the}$$
right hand column by the doubling process.

95 Magic squares revisited

This gives a nice starting point to investigate the idea of how transformations keep the magic property of a square invariant and leads to the idea of a group of transformations. But at one level it is just the interest in finding yet more magic squares which motivates this investigation.

There is much written on magic squares but the following references will make interesting reading:

Mathematical Activities by Brian Bolt
Magic Squares and Cubes by W S Andrews
Mathematical Recreations and Essays by W W Rouse Ball
Linear Algebra and its Applications by T J Fletcher
The Mathematical Gazette, No. 434, December 1981, an article by Brian S Reiner.

96 Do you know your birthday?

Children are always interested in finding out something about themselves so this activity motivates them. A calculator is not really needed, but should improve the chances of many children obtaining the correct answers –though they are more likely to make a mistake in calculating D by forgetting the numbers of days in each month. An easy question for children with a January birthday.

The way to appreciate how the method works is to note that, from one year to the next, Christmas Day (or any other date) advances by one week day only, except in a leap year when it advances by two week days. Now Y corresponds to the number of years, and X to the number of leap years from zero AD, so $Y + X$ corresponds to the advance in days of the week of a given date since zero AD. The method then assumes January 1st in the year 0 is a Friday and effectively works out the day for the date given in that year and its changes since then.

In practice of course the calendar has changed significantly over the years but the method is valid for any birthday in this century.

97 What scores are possible?

$$1 \quad 2 \quad 3 \quad \overset{\checkmark}{④} \quad 5 \quad 6 \quad 7 \quad \overset{\checkmark}{8} \quad 9 \quad 10 \quad \overset{\checkmark}{⑪} \quad \overset{\checkmark}{12} \quad \overset{?}{13} \quad \ldots$$

One approach to finding the obtainable totals is to argue that, up to 11, only multiples of 4 are possible. 11 and 12 are clearly possible. But for 13 to be possible it would have to be either 4 more than a previously obtained number, or 11 more than a previously obtained number. Now $13 - 4 = 9$ and $13 - 11 = 2$ which are not obtainable, so 13 is unobtainable. Similar arguments show that 14 is unobtainable, but 15 is obtainable as $15 - 4 = 11$. Pursuing this approach shows that 29 is unobtainable but then

$$30 = 2 \times \textcircled{11} + 2 \times \textcircled{4}$$
$$31 = \qquad \textcircled{11} + 5 \times \textcircled{4}$$
$$32 = \qquad\qquad 8 \times \textcircled{4}$$
$$33 = 3 \times \textcircled{11}$$

give four consecutive obtainable numbers. It follows that the next four numbers must be obtainable since

$$34 = 30 + 4 \qquad 35 = 31 + 4 \qquad 36 = 32 + 4$$
$$37 = 33 + 4$$

and then the next four, and so on, showing by an inductive argument that all the numbers greater than 29 can be obtained.

The unobtainable totals are:

1, 2, 3, 5, 6, 7, 9, 10, 13, 14, 17, 18, 21, 22, 25, 29

In general, when m and n have no common factor other than 1, the largest unobtainable total will be

$$mn - m - n$$

However, when m and n have a factor d only numbers which are multiples of d are obtainable so there is no largest unobtainable total. The proof of the above formula is beyond the scope of this book but the following analysis of the given example gives an indication of how the result may be justified.

Using 4 on its own any multiple of 4 can be obtained. It remains to show that by adding in multiples of 11 all the other numbers can be obtained after some point.

$$\text{Now} \qquad 11 = 2 \times 4 + 3$$
$$22 = 5 \times 4 + 2$$
$$\text{and} \qquad 33 = 8 \times 4 + 1$$

Thus the first three multiples of 11 differ from multiples of 4 by 3, 2 and 1 respectively. Hence by adding 4 onto them it is possible to achieve numbers of the form

$$4n + 3 \qquad 4n + 2 \qquad 4n + 1$$

Thus from 33 onwards all totals are possible. A little

thought will show that the largest unobtainable number occurs 4 short of 33 and is of the form

$$(4 - 1) 11 - 4$$

which more generally becomes

$$(n - 1) m - n \quad = \quad nm - m - n$$

Further reading on this activity may be found in the following copies of the *Mathematical Gazette*: Oct 1976 p. 219, Dec 1981 p. 239, Dec 1982 p. 302.

98 The elusive digit

The only digits missing from the results given are 0 and 3. The addition of the units digit in the first calculation given suggests the possibility that 3 may have been replaced by 7, and this is indeed the case.

The actual calculations were in fact

$$5\,6\,3\,2 + 7\,3\,4\,3 = 1\,2\,9\,7\,5$$
$$2\,3\,9 \times \quad 3\,6\,7 = 8\,7\,7\,1\,3$$

99 Chains of cube sums

All multiples of 3 end with 153. The diagram on page 174 shows the routes they take to this goal.

Table showing end points of cube sums for 1 to 99

		UNITS DIGIT									
		0	1	2	3	4	5	6	7	8	9
T	0		1	371	153		371	153			153
E	1	1	371	153		371	153				370
N	2	371	153		371	153					
S	3	153		371	153				370		
	4		371	153					407		
D	5	371	153								
I	6	153									
G	7				370	407					
I	8										407
T	9		370						407		

Most numbers of the form $3n - 1$ end with 371, but five 2-digit numbers of this set end with 407.

Numbers which are of the form $3n + 1$ do not always end with a single number, but with a cycle of numbers. For example:

$$22 \longrightarrow 16 \longrightarrow 217$$

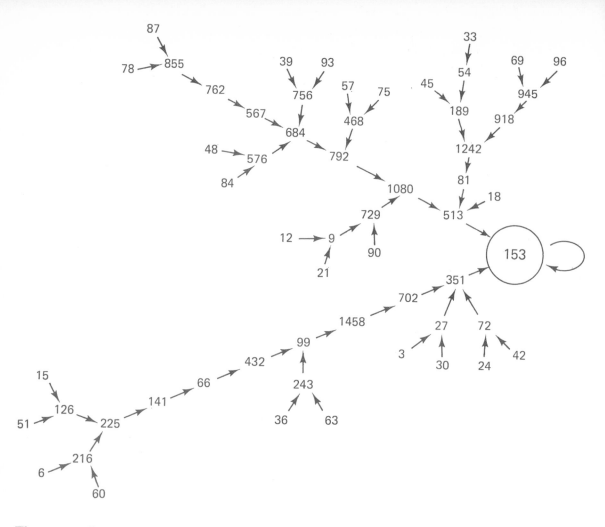

The arrow diagram is a very clear way of recording the chain, but you might also use a table like the one shown, partly completed.

100 Prime magic

1669	199	1249
619	1039	1459
829	1879	409

47	29	101
113	59	5
17	89	71

The solution to the given magic square is as above. It is easy to complete using the fact that the magic total is always three times the number in the centre square.

To find further prime magic squares you will first need

to construct a table of prime numbers, up to 300 say, and look for regular patterns of numbers to fulfil the criteria necessary to form a square. There is a good discussion of 3×3 squares and of prime numbers in *Mathematical Activities* by Brian Bolt.

The second magic square shown here has the smallest magic total for a set of prime numbers found by the author at the date of publication. He would like to hear from you if you find a smaller one. Remember 1 is not a prime number.

Four further solutions are shown below:

109	7	103
67	73	79
43	139	37

107	131	29
11	89	167
149	47	71

157	181	43
13	127	241
211	73	97

277	31	163
43	157	271
151	283	37

101 Surprise, surprise!

Any 6-digit number of the form *abc abc* is equivalent to $1000 \times abc + 1 \times abc$, that is $1001 \times abc$.
But $1001 = 13 \times 7 \times 11$.

There never will be a remainder.

102 Identical twins, quads and triplets

$49 \times \quad 101 = 4949$
$38 \times 10101 = 383838$
Now $10101 = 3 \times 7 \times 13 \times 37$

so any 2-digit number *ab* multiplied by 3 then 7 then 13 then 37 will give *ababab*.

$$73 \times 101 \times 137 = 1010101$$

so the product of *ab* by these numbers produces *abababab*.

103 Squares and cubes

$$2^2 + 2^2 = 2^3 \qquad\qquad 18^2 + 26^2 = 10^3$$
$$2^2 + 11^2 = 5^3 \qquad\qquad 16^2 + 16^2 = 8^3$$
$$5^2 + 10^2 = 5^3 \qquad\qquad 26^2 + 39^2 = 13^3$$
$$10^2 + 30^2 = 10^3 \qquad\qquad 9^2 + 46^2 = 13^3$$

Further, $2^3 + 2^3 = 4^2$

In five of the above sets the three numbers concerned have a common factor, so it suggests a consideration of numbers of the form $a = kp$ and $b = kq$. Then

$$a^2 + b^2 = (kp)^2 + (kq)^2 = k^2(p^2 + q^2)$$

Now this can be made into a perfect cube by making $p^2 + q^2 = k$, which leads to the identity

$$[p(p^2 + q^2)]^2 + [q(p^2 + q^2)]^2 = (p^2 + q^2)^3$$

and hence, by taking

$$a = p(p^2 + q^2) \qquad b = q(p^2 + q^2) \qquad c = p^2 + q^2$$

it will be true that $a^2 + b^2 = c^3$ for all values p and q.

The following table shows how this works out:

p	q	a	b	c
1	1	2	2	2
1	2	5	10	5
1	3	10	30	10
1	4	17	68	17
1	5	26	130	26
2	2	16	16	8
2	3	26	39	13
2	4	40	80	20
2	5	58	145	29

These formulae do not generate all possible solutions but the missing ones can be generated by taking

$$a = p(p^2 - 3q^2) \qquad b = q(3p^2 - q^2) \qquad c = p^2 + q^2$$

For example, when $p = 2$ and $q = 1$ this gives $a = 2$, $b = 11$ and $c = 5$.

104 Calculator golf

The skill comes in setting up an appropriate set of cards.
These must be devised with a particular set of players in
mind so the problems are understood, and not too trivial
or too difficult. However, as a calculator is being used, a
group of players with a wide range of ability could take
part by using a handicapping system as in real golf.

Producing many sets of cards would clearly be a big
task, but it should not be too difficult to produce a 9-hole
course on a sheet of paper, to Banda or photocopy.

Getting the players to record their estimates is helpful
and having foursomes with pairs of players playing other
pairs works well.

106 All present

$11\ 826^2 = 139\ 854\ 276$ $19\ 377^2 = 375\ 468\ 129$
$12\ 543^2 = 157\ 326\ 849$ $19\ 629^2 = 385\ 297\ 641$
$15\ 681^2 = 245\ 893\ 761$ $23\ 178^2 = 537\ 219\ 684$
$18\ 072^2 = 326\ 597\ 184$ $29\ 034^2 = 842\ 973\ 156$

Squaring the number as given in your calculator will
probably give the first seven digits correctly. Then squaring
the last two digits will give the final two digits of the
product.

A similar approach can be used with the difference of
the square numbers.
Alternatively use $a^2 - b^2 = (a + b)(a - b)$.

$11\ 113^2 - 200^2 = 123\ 458\ 769$
$11\ 115^2 - 294^2 = 123\ 456\ 789$
$31\ 111^2 - 200^2 = 967\ 854\ 321$
$191\ 161^2 - 188\ 560^2 = 987\ 654\ 321$

As $1 + 2 + 3 + 4 + \ldots + 9 = 45$ and 45 is divisible by
3, all such numbers have a factor of 3 so none of them is
prime.

107 Postage due

This is a puzzle based on the investigation in Activity 97.
What scores are possible?

Let $mn - m - n = 39$
then $(m - 1)(n - 1) = 40$
Thus $(m - 1)(n - 1) = 1 \times 40$ or 2×20 or 4×10 or
$$5 \times 8.$$

This leads to

$$(m, n) = (2,41) \text{ or } (3,21) \text{ or } (5,11) \text{ or } (6,9).$$

Of these possibilities (3,21) and (6,9) are clearly not correct for 39 would be obtainable.

However with stamps of denominations 2p and 41p *or* 5p and 11p the largest unobtainable postage would be 39p. Both solutions are correct although the second solution seems more realistic.

108 Ann's tower

The only way Ann could have made exactly three cubes of bricks from one cube of bricks is if the cubes in the tower have edges of 5 bricks, 4 bricks and 3 bricks and the box has an edge equivalent to 6 bricks for

$$3^3 + 4^3 + 5^3 = 6^3$$

and no other reasonably sized numbers satisfy this relationship.

The tower will be twelve bricks, i.e. 60 cm, high.

109 Reconstructing the manor house

54 ft by 24 ft by 12 ft

If the length, breadth and height of the room are a, b and c feet respectively, then

$$ac = 648 \qquad bc = 288 \qquad ab = 1296$$

from which $\quad c^2 = \dfrac{ac.bc}{ab} = \dfrac{648 \times 288}{1296} = 144$

giving $\qquad c = 12 \text{ ft}$

Then $\qquad a = \dfrac{ac}{c} = \dfrac{648}{12} = 54 \text{ ft}$

and $\qquad b = \dfrac{bc}{c} = \dfrac{288}{12} = 24 \text{ ft}$

110 The blanket box

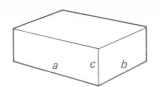

$a = 72$ cm
$b = 45$ cm
$c = 39$ cm

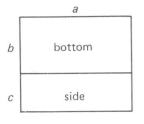

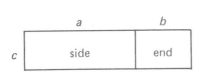

The dimensions may be found by trial and error but can be approached analytically as follows.

Let the dimensions be a, b, c as shown and let the areas of the three pieces of plywood be X, Y and Z respectively, then

$$X = a + b \qquad Y = ac + bc \qquad Z = ab + bc$$

so $\quad \frac{1}{2}(X + Y - Z) = ac \quad \frac{1}{2}(Y + Z - X) = bc \quad \frac{1}{2}(Z + X - Y) = ab$

Use $\frac{ac.bc}{ab}$ to find c and then the other two dimensions are easily determined, see Activity 109, Reconstructing the manor house.

112 Topsy-turvy

If $abc \ldots k \times 9 = k \ldots cba$ then it is easy to see that $a = 1$ and $k = 9$, for any other value of a would lead to a number being carried, and hence generating a number involving more digits than the original.

But $19 \times 9 \neq 91$ because of the 8 to be carried when multiplying the 9 in the units column by 9.

Consideration of $1b9 \times 9$ soon shows that it cannot be equal to $9b1$ again because of the carry over.

However, consideration of

$$1\,b\,c\,9 \times 9 = 9\,c\,b\,1$$

soon leads to the fact that $b = 0$ and then $c = 8$ satisfies the given requirements.

$$1089 \times 9 = 9801$$

This is the smallest solution, and the only one with 4 digits.

The next three solutions are

10 989	5 digits
109 989	6 digits
1 099 989	7 digits.

Then, with an obvious pattern emerging, there are two solutions with 8 digits, namely

10 999 989   and   10 891 089.

and again with 9 digits:

109 999 989   and   108 901 089.

With 10 digits three solutions are possible

1 099 999 989   1 089 001 089   1 098 910 989

but these build on existing solutions and no new principle is required to find the solutions with any number of digits.

The numbers whose digits are reversed by multiplying by 4 are closely related to the above – in fact are all double the above.

$$1\ 089 \times 2 = 2\ 178 \quad \text{and} \quad 2\ 178 \times 4 = 8\ 712$$
$$10\ 989 \times 2 = 21\ 978 \quad \text{and} \quad 21\ 978 \times 4 = 87\ 912$$

and so on.

113 Divisibility

A very good investigation which requires and reinforces the use of divisibility tests. The 5, for example, must be in the middle, for no other five-digit number constructed from the digits 1, 2, . . ., 9 is divisible by 5. As all the digits sum to 45, and this is divisible by 9, any order for the digits will always be divisible by 9 so divisibility by 9 can be taken for granted. The sum of the first six digits must be divisible by 3 and the sixth digit must be even for the number formed from the first six digits to be divisible by 6. In fact every other digit must be even for the required divisibility by 2, 4, 6 and 8.

Such arguments as the foregoing help considerably, but use of the calculator and a certain amount of trial and error will be required to find the number divisible by 7.

There is only one solution: 381 654 729.

But be warned of too much dependence on your calculator. If it only displays 8 digits then 963 258 147 will appear to be a solution for it will appear that 96 325 814 is divisible by 8 . . . but this is impossible as 814 does not divide by 8.

114 Calculator challenges

1 $2025 = 45^2$ $3136 = 56^2$
   $2025 + 1111 = 3136$ and further $45 + 11 = 56$.
2 $65^2 - 56^2 = 33^2$.
3 This property of square numbers follows from

$$(a^2 + b^2)(c^2 + d^2) = (ac + bd)^2 + (ad - bc)^2.$$

But there is always a second possibility for

$$(a^2 + b^2)(c^2 + d^2) = (ac - bd)^2 + (ad + bc)^2.$$

For anyone with a knowledge of complex numbers these identities can be deduced from

$$(a + ib)(c + id) = (ac - bd) + (ad + bc)\,i$$
$$\text{and } (a - ib)(c + id) = (ac + bd) + (ad - bc)\,i.$$

115 The Giant and the Dwarfs

With the given starting position the dwarfs should win by trapping the giant in circle 5, but one false move and he can slip past them.

With other starting positions the advantage can change in the giant's favour. For example, if the dwarfs start as in the diagram but the giant starts on square 1 then the giant should win. See if you can decide which starting positions ensure a win for the dwarfs (always assuming they use the right tactics) and which favour the giant.

116 Rhyme around

Both rhymes are aids to remembering the digits for an approximation to π. Count the number of letters in each word . . .
$\pi = 3.141\ 529\ 653\ 589\ 793\ 238\ 46 \ldots$

117 The Ruby wedding

A puzzle based on Pythagorean triples. The Ruby wedding celebration puts the likely ages of William and Ruth above 56, while their ages are not likely to differ by more than one if they shared a desk at school. This suggests numbers which differ by one whose squares differ by a square number.

Now $61^2 - 60^2 = 11^2$
and $85^2 - 84^2 = 13^2$

look likely. The second can be ruled out however as it suggests a family of thirteen children born to a couple who married in their forties. Thus William and 'young Ruth' married when they were 21 and 20 respectively, and raised eleven children.

118 The medieval courtyard

The sides of the courtyard are approximately 56.54 m.

A deceptively easy problem, it can be solved by use of Pythagoras' theorem, algebraic manipulation, and a calculator. From the diagram:

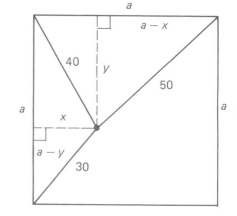

$$x^2 + (a - y)^2 = 900 \qquad (1)$$
$$(a - x)^2 + y^2 = 2500 \qquad (2)$$
$$x^2 + y^2 = 1600 \qquad (3)$$

(1) $-$ (3) gives $a^2 - 2ay + 700 = 0$ (4)
(2) $-$ (3) gives $a^2 - 2ax - 900 = 0$ (5)

Substituting from (4) and (5) for y and x in (3) leads to

$$a^4 - 3400a^2 + 650\,000 = 0$$

which can first be solved as a quadratic in a^2.

119 Fill the gaps

There are theoretically an infinite number of possibilities and the point of this activity is to emphasise that there are many ways of completing a sequence.

(a) 1, 4, 7, 10, 13, 16, 19. Add 3
(b) 1, 2, 4, 7, 11, 16, 22. Add 1 more each time.
(c) 1, 6, 3, 10, 7, 16, 13. Two sets of differences involved:
Adding 5, 7, 9, . . . and taking away 3.

The difference between 1 and 16 is 15 so one way of generating the sequence is to find a pattern of five differences whose sum is 15. For example, the pattern 1, 6, 1, 6, 1 sums to 15 and leads to the sequence

1, 2, 8, 9, 15, 16

Similarly, 7, −3, 7, −3, 7 sums to 15 and gives the sequence

1, 8, 5, 12, 9, 16 and so on.

120 Find the route

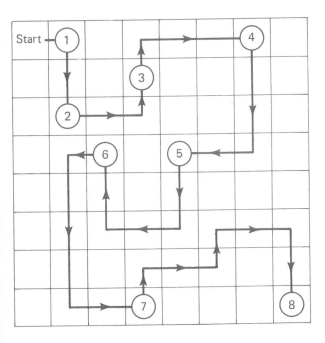

The solution shown here is the one around which the puzzle was built. Clearly with these numbers there are many alternative routes. There may be other solutions using numbers in different squares but they were not planned!

Much patience, and a systematic search starting from both ends of the route are probably the main ingredients for solving this puzzle. It is however relatively easy to set similar ones and this in itself is a worthwhile activity.

121 501 up!

An interesting exercise in prime numbers.
The three highest scores are

167 = treble 20 + treble 19 + bull
157 = bull + bull + treble 19
151 = treble 19 + treble 18 + double 20.

As $501 = 3 \times 167$ it could take only three turns to reach this total if the thrower is very skilful.

As the score of 167 cannot be achieved in a turn where a dart enters the double ring it will be necessary to start the fifth turn. Further, as the fourth turn must be odd if it is prime, this also leaves an odd total for the fifth turn which cannot be achieved with less than 2 darts if it is to end in a double. One way of achieving the total of 501 with fourteen darts is as follows:

1st turn	treble 20 + treble 19 + bull	167
2nd turn	treble 20 + treble 19 + bull	167
3rd turn	treble 20 + treble 20 + 7	127
4th turn	20 + 15 + 2	37
5th turn	1 + double 1	3
		501

Here is one way of reaching zero with nine darts where the running total is always prime.

```
              501
        −  170  = treble 20 + treble 20 + bull
prime     331
        −  180  = 3 × treble 20
prime     151
        −  151  = treble 20 + treble 17 + double 20
             0
```

122 One, two, three, four, five ...

This game encourages students to explore the
characteristics of the different functions on their calculator.
For example, the CASIO HL-807 has a constant function
so that

$$1 + = = = = \boxed{MR}$$

will give 4 in the display, or a number n equal to the
number of times the '=' key is pressed.

The use of a memory will also give simple solutions
although not necessarily the most efficient. Thus
$$1 \boxed{M+} \boxed{M+} \boxed{M+} \boxed{M+} \boxed{M+} \boxed{M+} \boxed{MR}$$
gives 6 with 8 key presses
but $1 + 2 + 3 =$
gives   6 with 6 key presses
as does $1 \times 2 \times 3 =$
or $1 + 2 = = \boxed{MR}$ (in a CASIO HL 807)
or $1 + 2 = \boxed{INV}\boxed{x!}$
The following give solutions to the first 20 but are not
necessarily the best!

		No of key presses
1:	1	1
2:	1×2	3
3:	$1 + 2 =$	4
4:	$1 \times 2 \times =$	5
5:	$\cdot 1 \boxed{1/x} \div 2 =$	6
6:	$1 \times 2 \times 3 =$	6
7:	$1 + 2 \times 3 =$	6 (on Casio fx $-$ 8100)
8:	$\cdot 1 \boxed{1/x} - 2 =$	6
9:	$1 + 2 = \times =$	6
10:	$\cdot 1 \boxed{1/x}$	3
11:	$1 - 2 + 3 \times 4 =$	8
12:	$\cdot 1 \boxed{1/x} + 2 =$	6
13:	$1 + 2 \boxed{x^y} 3 + 4 =$	8
14:	$1 \times 2 + 3 \times 4 =$	8
15:	$\cdot 1 \boxed{1/x} \div 2 \times 3 =$	8
16:	$1 \times 2 \times = \times =$	7
17:	$\cdot 1 \; 1/x \times 2 - 3 =$	8
18:	$1 + 2 = \times = \boxed{M+}\boxed{M+}\boxed{MR}$	9
19:	$1 \times 2 \times = \times = + 3 =$	10
20:	$\cdot 1 \boxed{1/x} \times 2 =$	6

123 Crossed ladders

This is an old chestnut which is not nearly as easy as it looks.

Using Pythagoras' theorem

$$AC^2 = 10^2 - a^2 = 8 - b^2$$

so $a^2 - b^2 = 36$ (1)

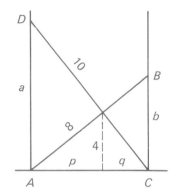

Using similar triangles

$$\frac{4}{a} = \frac{q}{p+q} \qquad \frac{4}{b} = \frac{p}{p+q}$$

so $\frac{4}{a} + \frac{4}{b} = 1$ (2)

Rearranging (2) gives

$$b = \frac{4a}{a-4}$$

and substituting in (1) gives

$$a^2 - \left(\frac{4a}{a-4}\right)^2 = 36$$

which leads to the quartic equation

$$a^4 - 8a^3 - 36a^2 + 288a - 576 = 0$$

Solution by trial and error or more sophisticated numerical techniques leads to

$$9.25 < a < 9.255$$

from which $AC \doteqdot 3.8\text{m}$

A similar problem which is easy to state but even harder to solve is that of finding the length of the tether of a goat attached to a ring at the edge of a circular field so that the goat has access to only half the field!

124 Target

This need not be played as a competitive game – individuals enjoy the challenge of finding routes to the target on their own. It could become a class activity over a period of time with the different routes found being added to a wall chart.

One point to watch is that calculators differ in their logic so the same set of key presses can lead to different results on different calculators and cause confusion initially. For example, on a CASIO HL 807

gives 80 in the display, but on a CASIO fx−8100 the same sequence gives 66. Be warned!

125 One and zeros

(a) $100 - 11 - 11 - 1 =$ 12 key presses

   or $10 - 1 - 1 - 1 \times 11 =$

(b) $100 - 11 \times 11 =$ 10 key presses

Some scientific calculators give -21 as a result of this
sequence of key presses, however, so the best sequence
then is probably

$100 - 11 = \times 11 =$

   or $1000 - 11 - 10 =$ 11 key presses

(c) $11 \times = \times 11 + 101 =$ 12 key presses

(d) $100 - 11$ $\boxed{M+}$ $\boxed{MR}$ $\boxed{M+}$ $\boxed{MR}$ $\times 11 =$

14 key presses

(e) $1 + 1$ $\boxed{M+}$ $\boxed{x^y}$ $11 -$ $\boxed{MR}$ $=$ 10 key presses

(f) $11 + 1\times = \times 111 - 1 =$ 13 key presses

In checking these with your calculator you might not get
the right answer. Different answers achieved by the same
sequence of key presses even with calculators of the same
make are an occupational hazard – make sure you know
your own calculator. For example on two Casio calculators
used by the author one interprets the sequence

$a - b \times c$

as $(a - b) \times c$ and the other as $a - (b \times c)$.

126 A cautionary tale

This is an example of what mathematicians call ill-
conditioned equations. As given, the solution of the
equations is

$x = 1776$ $y = -4186,$

but as given in the textbook the solution would be

$x = -770$ $y = 1816.$

Thought of as equations of straight lines it will be seen that
their gradients are very nearly equal: -2.3585 and
-2.3581 to 4 dp thus the slightest change of the gradient
of one line radically changes the point of intersection of
the two lines.

127 Another calculator crossword

1. H	I	**2.** L	L	■	**3.** S	O	**4.** B
O	■	E	■	**5.** H	I	■	O
S	■	S	■	**6.** E	G	G	S
7. E	L	L	**8.** I	E	■	H	S
■	■	**9.** I	S	L	**10.** E	**11.** G	■
12. O	■	**13.** E	L	S	E	**14.** O	**15.** H
I	■	E	■	**16.** L	O	B	E
17. L	O	O	S	E	■	I	■

The following list of calculator words is not complete but gives some idea of what is possible. It ignores plurals where just an 's' is required.

B.	be	G.	geese	I.	I	S.	see
	bee		gel		Ibo		seize
	Bee Gees		gibe		igloo		sell
	beg		gig		ill		she
	bell		giggle		is		shell
	Bess		Giles		isle		shoe
	Bessie		Gill				siege
	bib		gillie	L.	lee		sigh
	Bible		glebe		leg		sill
	big		glee		Leo		silo
	bile		glib		Leslie		sizzle
	bilges		globe		less		sleigh
	Bill		gloss		Libbie		slob
	bless		go		lie		sloe
	bliss		gob		Lil		slog
	blob		gobble		Lille		slosh
	Bob		Gobi		lillies		so
	Bobbie		goes		Lilo		sob
	bobsleigh		goggle		Lisle		Soh
	bog		goose		Liz		soil
	boggle		gosh		Lizzie		sole
	bogle				lo		solo
	boil	H.	he		Lob		SOS
	boo		heel		lobe		
	boob		hell		log	Z.	Zoe
	booze		hello		loll		zoo
	bosh		high		lollies		
	boss		hill		loo		
			his		Looe		
E.	ebb		hiss		loose		
	eel		ho		lose		
	egg		hob		loss		
	eh		hobbies				
	Elbe		hobble	O.	obese		
	Eli		hobo		oblige		
	Ellie		hoe		oboe		
	else		hog		ogle		
	Elsie		hole		oh		
	Esso		hose		oil		
					ooze		
					Oslo		

FURTHER RESOURCES

Books

W. S. Andrews, *Magic Squares and Cubes* (Dover)

B. Averbach and O. Chein, *Mathematics: Problem Solving Through Recreational Mathematics* (W.H. Freeman)

D. St. P. Barnard, *Figure it Out* (Pan)

Stephen Barr, *Experiments in Topology* (John Murray)

A. H. Beiler, *Recreations in the Theory of Numbers* (Dover)

David Bergamini, *Mathematics* (Life Science Library)

E. R. Berlekamp, J. H. Conway and R. K. Guy, *Winning Ways* (Academic Press)

Pierre Berloquin, *Geometric Games* (Unwin Paperbacks)

A. B. Bolt, *We Built Our Own Computers* (Cambridge University Press)

A. B. Bolt and J. E. Hiscocks, *Machines, Mechanisms and Mathematics* (Chatto and Windus for the Schools Council Mathematics for the Majority Project)

Brian Bolt, *Mathematical Activities* (Cambridge University Press)

Edward de Bono, *The Five-Day Course in Thinking* (Pelican)

R. Courant and H. Robbins, *What is Mathematics?* (Oxford University Press)

H. M. Cundy and A. P. Rollet, *Mathematical Models* (Oxford University Press)

H. E. Dudeney, *Amusements in Mathematics* (Dover)

H. E. Dudeney, *The Canterbury Puzzles* (Dover)

H. E. Dudeney, *Puzzles and Curious Problems* (Fontana)

Edward B. Edwards, *Pattern and Design with Dynamic Symmetry* (Dover)

The Graphic Work of M. C. Escher (Pan)

J. Ewing and C. Kosniowski, *Puzzle it out: Cubes, Groups and Puzzles* (Cambridge University Press)

T. J. Fletcher, *Linear Algebra and its Applications*

P. French and R. J. Rickard, *Exploring Mathematics,* a series of enrichment booklets (McGraw-Hill)

Aaron J. Friedland, *Puzzles in Mathematics and Logic* (Dover)

R. Buckminster Fuller and R. W. Marks, *The Dymaxion World of Buckminster Fuller* (Doubleday)

G. Gamow and M. Stern, *Puzzle-math* (Macmillan)

Martin Gardner, *Mathematical Puzzles and Diversions* (Pelican)

Martin Gardner, *More Mathematical Puzzles and Diversions* (Pelican)

Martin Gardner, *Further Mathematical Diversions* (Pelican)

Martin Gardner, *Mathematical Carnival* (Pelican)

Martin Gardner, *Mathematical Circus* (Pelican)

Martin Gardner, *Mathematics, Magic and Mystery* (Pelican)

Martin Gardner, *New Mathematical Diversions* (Allen and Unwin)

Solomon W. Golomb, *Polyominoes* (Allen and Unwin)

L. A. Graham, *Ingenious Mathematical Problems and Methods* (Dover)

Gerald Jenkins and Anne Wild, *Make Shapes,* Series no. 1, no. 2 and no. 3 (Tarquin Publications)

E. Kasner and J. Newman, *Mathematics and the Imagination* (Bell)

E. H. Lockwood, *A Book of Curves* (Cambridge University Press)

Lorraine Mottershead, *Sources of Mathematical Discovery* (Basil Blackwell)

E. P. Northrop, *Riddles in Mathematics* (Pelican)

H. Phillips, *My Best Puzzles in Mathematics* (Dover)

W. W. Rouse Ball, *Mathematical Recreations and Essays* (Macmillan)

Royal Vale Heath, *Mathemagic* (Dover)

Doris Schattschneider and Wallace Walker, *M. C. Escher Kaleidocycles* (Tarquin Publications)

Schools Council Mathematics for the Majority Project, *Machines, Mechanisms and Mathematics* (Chatto and Windus)

Dale Seymour, *Sum Puzzles* (Creative Publications, Inc.)

H. Steinhaus, *Mathematical Snapshots* (Oxford University Press)

H. Steinhaus, *One Hundred Problems in Elementary Mathematics* (Pergamon)

P. van Delft and J. Botermans, *Creative Puzzles of the World* (Cassell)

Magazines

Factor, produced for children by teachers through the SMILE Centre, Middle Row School, Kensal Road, London W10

Mathematical Pie, also published for children, available from West View, Fiveways, Warwick

Hypotenuse, a mathematics journal for secondary school students whose contributions are largely from the

students themselves, available from Explorers Unlimited,
Four Gables, Village Road, Denham, Bucks UB9 5BN

Mathematics in School, for secondary and middle school
teachers, and

The Mathematical Gazette, mainly for sixth form teachers,
both published by The Mathematical Association, 259
London Road, Leicester LE2 3BE

Mathematics Teaching, for school teachers at all levels, and
published by the Association of Teachers of
Mathematics, King's Chamber, Queen Street, Derby,
DE1 3DA

Teaching Mathematics and its Applications, for secondary
teachers is published by the Institute of Mathematics and
its Applications, Maitland House, Warrior Square,
Southend-on-Sea, Essex, SS1 2JY

The Arithmetic Teacher and *The Mathematics Teacher*
both published by the National Council of Teachers of
Mathematics, 1906 Association Drive, Reston, Virginia
22091, USA

Games

Amoeba (Louis Marx)
Archimedes (Invicta)
Backgammon
Battleship (MB)
Black Box (Waddingtons)
Blockbuster (D. Cross, School of Education, Exeter
University)
Check Lines (Tri-ang)
Chess
Cluedo (Waddingtons)
Connect 4 (Milton Bradley)
Cover-up (Ideal)
Dominoes
Draughts
Erector 500 (Ideal)
Four Sight (Invicta)
Fox and Geese (Galt toys)
Go
Harmonograph (Peter Pan Playthings)
Hexagonal Chess
Hi-Q Euclid (Peter Pan Playthings)
Hi-Q Pythagoras (Peter Pan Playthings)
Impuzzables (Cube puzzles by Action GT)
Interaction (Waddingtons)
Kensington
Lego

L-Game (de Bono)
Magic Cube (Pentangle)
Mancala (Spear's Games)
Master Mind (Invicta)
Meccano
Monopoly (Waddingtons)
Nine Men's Morris
Noughts and Crosses in three dimensions (various
  commercial forms, e.g. Fours, and Space Lines)
Othello (Peter Pan Playthings)
Pick a Pair! 30 board games for 2 players (A. and C.
  Black Ltd)
Reversi (Spear's Games)
Shinsei Mystery
Skirrid (Eliot-Taylor)
Snooker
Solitaire
Spirograph (Denys Fisher)
Squares (Waddingtons)
Stay Alive (MB)
Take Two! 32 board games for 2 players (A. and C. Black
  Ltd)
Tot-ten (Spear's Games)
Touch Down (Invicta–formerly marketed as Pressups)
Trap (Ideal)
Tricky Button Puzzles
Trimatics (Spear's Games)

Some useful sources of games and puzzles are:

Double Games Ltd, 10 Hampstead Gardens, London NW11
Games Centre, 16 Hamway Street, London W1A 2LS
Pentangle, Over Wallop, Hants SO20 8NT

INDEX